The
Sacred Thread

A TRUE STORY OF BECOMING

A MOTHER AND FINDING A FAMILY

——HALF A WORLD AWAY

The
Sacred Thread

Adrienne Arieff
with Beverly West

CROWN PUBLISHERS • NEW YORK

All rights reserved.
Published in the United States by Crown Publishers, an imprint of the Crown Publishing
Group, a division of Random House, Inc., New York.
www.crownpublishing.com

CROWN and the Crown colophon are registered trademarks of Random House, Inc.

Library of Congress Cataloging-in-Publication Data is available upon request.

ISBN 978-0-307-71668-2
eISBN 978-0-307-71670-5

Printed in the United States of America

BOOK DESIGN BY ELINA D. NUDELMAN
JACKET DESIGN BY NUPOOR GORDON
JACKET PHOTOGRAPHY © DINODIA IMAGES

10 9 8 7 6 5 4 3 2 1
First Edition

THIS BOOK IS DEDICATED TO MY FATHER, ALLEN, AND LATE MOTHER, CAROL, WHO BOTH TAUGHT ME TO FOLLOW MY DREAMS, NOT TO FEAR NEW THINGS, AND TO TREAT EVERY‹ ONE WITH RESPECT.

I HOPE THIS BOOK HELPS ANYONE WHO HAS EVER STRUGGLED WITH INFERTILITY.

AUTHOR'S NOTE

I have changed the names of some people in this book out of respect for their privacy. I have rearranged some instances and events. I have taken a few people I met along the way and condensed them into fewer people so as not to distract from the larger story. Otherwise, this book is a true account of my experiences as I remember them happening.

At one end of this world, there is one woman who desperately needs a baby and cannot have her own child. And at the other end, there is a woman who badly wants to help her own family. If these two women want to help each other, why not allow that? They're helping one another to have a new life in this world.

—Dr. Nayna Patel, medical director
Akanksha Infertility Clinic
Anand, India

THE SACRED THREAD

In the Hindu tradition, when a child is ready to leave home, join their guru, and begin their spiritual journey, a coming-of-age ceremony is performed. During the ritual known as the *Upanayana*, or the Sacred Thread, the child is given a cord composed of three strands, woven together and secured by a single knot. For the rest of their lives, Brahmans wear this thread, draped over the shoulder, as a physical representation of their umbilical connection to parents, God, and the world. No matter how far one travels from his or her origins, an undeniable connection remains. Also known as the Second Birth, the Sacred Thread ceremony is a celebration and an affirmation of the ties that anchor, guide, and connect us throughout our lives, dating back to Creation, and extending to Eternity.

The
Sacred Thread

chapter 1

I feel the heat first. It rouses me from disorienting, sticky dreams. The walls of my hotel room are an earthy reddish brown, like the interior of a tandoori oven—steamy, close, and designed to inten-sify and tenderize its contents. I'm slow-roasting. My thoughts are slow and muddy—this heat! How can anyone think in this heat?—and as I rub my eyes and look out my window, I remem-ber. *Oh my God, I'm in India!*

I've just traveled nine thousand miles to arrive here, a rural pocket of northern India near the border with Pakistan, to have a child. I have come here under the direction of a fertility spe-cialist to whom I've only spoken over the phone, to undergo IVF treatment and have children at last, with the help of an Indian surrogate I've never met. There is no guarantee that any of this will be successful.

I slide open my window to relieve the stifling heat in my room. This, it turns out, has the opposite effect. As hard as it is to imagine, it's actually hotter *outside*. While the inside of my room is baking, it is nothing compared to the sopping, still air of the street. The humidity is a wall on this windless day; the atmo-sphere is completely and eternally inert. These are the dog days of Indian summer.

When I open my window, I not only invite in the heat but also the carnival of life in the street. All five senses are immediately assailed with a riot of sensation—color, noise, pollution, heat, incense—and everywhere the incessant, high-volume hum and honk of village life.

There's no doubt about it, I'm not in the Bay Area anymore. The urban comforts I have come to rely on are nowhere in sight. My smartphone is perpetually losing signal, and I don't imagine that there is a latte or a martini or even a good roast chicken to be found within five hundred miles. Anand is a district located in the state of Gujarat, which is strictly vegetarian. No restaurant, hotel, or self-respecting citizen serves beef, pork, chicken, or fish, even to a foreigner like me. Gujarat is also a dry state, no alcohol allowed, though if I had a drink in this heat, I swear I might pass out. But, after the day I think I'm about to have, I might be willing to risk it.

I look up the street and then down, trying to get the lay of the land, but it's a jumbled puzzle of honking and yelling and rumbling, and unexplained explosions in the distance every now and again, explosions that nobody seems to pay much attention to. I can't make any sense of it. There are no cultural landmarks to guide me, no familiar sights, sounds, or smells. I feel as if I have been dropped on a foreign planet. A dry, screaming-hot planet with no cheeseburgers.

I sigh, turning back toward my cramped hotel room. I am, after all, a capable and well-traveled woman. While in college, I interned with the Peace Corps in Washington, D.C., and at an international telecommunications firm—both took me to places I had never dreamed I would get to visit, from Guatemala to Mexico City to Hong Kong. After graduation, I went to Israel and lived in a kibbutz for four months, and then was off to follow a Spanish boyfriend to Madrid.

This knowledge—the certainty that no matter how strange my surroundings, I will find friendship, laughter, and love—is the only thing that is giving me courage right now. I cling to these thin straws of strength; they are a raft in a vast and unfamiliar ocean.

Let's face it, I am embarking on a bold and frightening new adventure.

Right now I feel like I'm having an out-of-body experience, or that I am trapped in a foreign film without the benefit of subtitles. I feel numb, and nervous, but very excited too. My emotions are as chaotic as the traffic in the streets, all traveling at max capacity toward a head-on collision with the unknown.

Even though I've been on planes, trains, and automobiles to get here, the full weight of my passage and of what I hope to achieve in this journey has not quite resonated until now. I've held off the full awareness of what's happening until this, the absolute last moment. I have no choice but to go forward. Truthfully, I think I only made it this far by closing my eyes to the sheer madness of the adventure. When you're facing something as intractable and incomprehensible as infertility, and you're feeling helpless and hopeless, denial can be your best friend. It's what makes it possible to run where angels fear to tread. My mom taught me that. I thought she was crazy the first time she said it, but now I understand the method to her madness.

Three elephants lumber nonchalantly past my window. They are as unremarkable and routine a part of this landscape as the children skipping by on their way to school, or the tangle of traffic in the streets. Behind them are strutting, screaming peacocks pecking in the dust for a few breakfast crumbs. On the corner a group of sacred cows linger, superior and detached. Wagons rattle on their way to the old town market, weighed down with mangos, watermelons, bananas, jasmine, roses, handcrafts, and spices of all varieties. Whole families linger on the sidewalks, selling a few sparse wares—an embroidered pouch, a used tire, a flavored ice, or something fried—and letting the morning roll untroubled into afternoon beneath the relentless July sun.

I'm exploring a brand-new frontier of emotional and ethical hills and valleys, without a clue as to where I'm headed. Except for this: I know that at the other end lies the possibility that my husband, Alex, and I will become parents; that I will finally, after so many years, so many hopes, so many heartbreaks, become a mother. So I'm willing to take the journey, and write the map and the guidebook as I go.

I'm at peace with Alex's and with my decision ethically, spiritually, physically, and emotionally. I know in my gut, the way one does in watershed moments, that we're doing the right thing. No matter what happens, we will make sure that we take care of ourselves, our surrogate, and hopefully, our soon-to-be-born baby. And yet...

Oh my God, I'm in India!

chapter 2

The large wooden door of my hotel room swings open, and a man dressed in a crisp cotton dhoti steps in.

"Hello," he says, with a wide, friendly smile. "I am Abhi, your driver. I will take you to the clinic."

"Oh, great!" My pulse, much like the riptide of rickshaws outside my window, accelerates from 0 to 100 in a millisecond. It's actually happening. I'm going to the clinic! I finally calm down enough to realize that a strange man has just barged into my room without knocking. I'm not even dressed. "I'll be down, stairs in five minutes," I say, with a pinch of irritation. Is it customary to walk into a strange woman's room without knocking? And does my door *lock*?

"Yes, yes, yes," Abhi says.

He doesn't move an inch.

"I'll be downstairs in five minutes," I say, more loudly this time, thinking perhaps he hasn't heard me.

"True, true," Abhi says, still smiling, still not moving. I shrug my shoulders and go with the flow. After all, when in India . . .

I dash into the other room and change as quickly as I can into one of the light cotton outfits I've had specially made for the trip. From past experience with Indian summers, I knew that when in India it's best to dress the way the Indians do, in

Indian cotton so light it feels as if you are wearing nothing at all. When I emerge, Abhi appears to have gotten the message, and I find him waiting for me in the lobby. He leads me past the reception desk toward the car, opens the door for me, and gently helps me inside. Abhi still makes me a little nervous, but the Fates have appointed him as my escort into the unknown, so I decide to trust the universe. And besides, I have no other choice.

En route to the clinic, Abhi and I manage to communicate the important things between near misses with the haphazard jumble of vehicles that whiz by me on all sides. He is a quiet but congenial man. I learn that he is in his early forties. He served in the military with the clinic's director, Dr. Nayna Patel's husband, Hitesh, who he says at one point saved his life. He has been working at the clinic ever since, and Abhi and Hitesh are dear friends. He is devoted to his wife and children, and is originally from Anand, of which he seems enormously proud.

"This is my city. Gotchit? You understand me?" He gestures expansively to the right and to the left, and points out highlights as we drive through his hometown, laughing perpetually. "My town!"

"Yes, got it!" I say, shaking my head affirmatively so hard I feel like a bobble head on Abhi's dashboard. We turn onto Anand's equivalent of Main Street. Animals and people and vehicles, all manner of creatures on four legs or two, a vast variety of wares—all are jammed into this one narrow dirt lane. I feel like a fish being guided and directed by the will of the school rather than by my own individual agenda. Just before we are completely swallowed up by the current, Abhi blows his horn several times, shouts a few things out the window, accompanied by a gesture that I don't understand, and turns to me, smiling triumphantly, as the seas part. I wonder what he has said that has had such an effect on man and beast alike, but I don't have much time to ponder as we are almost rear-ended by a wagon full of Indian textiles, and I imagine myself buried in Varanasi brocades and pashmina shawls. Tailgating seems to be a recreational sport in Anand. The wagon swerves around us at the last moment and trundles toward the market, and we turn off onto a quieter side street, heading out of the center of town, toward the clinic.

"Lovely town," I say, still rattled from my near miss with death by pashmina, and the kinetic syncopation of the unpaved lane that was bouncing me all over the backseat. "So many people and so many . . . *cows!*"

Abhi laughs. "Ches!" he says. "Lotsa holy cows!"

❀⋙✥⋘❀

Anand is a small village in the north of the country, where tourists rarely venture. It's the milk capital of India, and is famous throughout the country for its ice cream, its agricultural college, and its complete disregard of traffic laws. Most recently, it has also become the capital of foreign gestational surrogacy, and clinics are springing up everywhere, along with attendant billboards advertising their services.

Regulations still lag behind the scope of the services being offered, and for now, the town itself still looks like the sleepy and forgotten place it was before the clinics came. The highlights of Anand are the ice cream parlor, the tearoom, the hotel I am staying in, and the new vegetarian Pizza Hut that just opened down the road, to much excitement.

Foreign gestational surrogacy is big business, however, and ultimately it will change life in this small town. Hundreds of thousands of dollars have already flowed through Anand in a very short space of time, and business is expected to quadruple in the next few years.

There is construction going on everywhere here, and there are more and more town cars sprinkled in amongst the ram, shackle rickshaws, driving Western couples from the airport to the clinics and back again with babies in their arms. Luxury hotels will soon go up to accommodate the new foreign traffic. Restaurants and fitness clubs and juice bars and newsstands will be soon to follow. Anand is already changing—but Anand doesn't want to know it yet.

You can almost feel the tension that comes from sudden economic expansion rumbling in the earth beneath your feet. It's as if everyone knows that the ground is moving, and they aren't quite sure how they feel about it. But in India in the last half century, change happens, no matter how anybody feels about it. In India, the earth moves of its own accord, and people do their best to adapt.

❊❀❊❀❊

Finally, we turn onto a cramped cul de sac, and the Akanksha Infertility Clinic comes into view for the first time. The clinic is a modest concrete three-story building, virtually surrounded by families of beggars and the inevitable, ubiqui, tous cows meditating in the blast furnace of high noon in Anand. The building is badly in need of a makeover. An unfortunate combination of beige and light peach collide haphazardly on the exterior walls, and there are some rather grave-looking cracks in the concrete entranceway steps that make me question the strength of the foundation. The building looks like it should be closed for remodeling, and it's far from clean. I had not yet learned one of the great lessons of India: You can't judge a book by its cover.

Abhi doesn't seem at all put off by the ragtag welcoming committee at the front door, and bounds out of the driver's seat, pulling me excitedly out of the car, then pushing me gently but firmly through the doors before I can change my mind. As the head driver for the Akanksha Clinic, Abhi has obviously done this very same kindness many times before. He is adept at dealing with women who, like me, are prone to feeling a little rattled at the outset, and he instinctually understands the power of pacing when it comes to managing panic.

Once inside, the atmosphere is notably calmer, but still I'm a bit concerned. I've come to this clinic to undergo medical procedures myself, and I expect a certain level of courtesy, not to mention hygiene. I knew I wasn't going to Cedars-Sinai, but I had anticipated at least a fresh coat of paint.

"May I help you?" the nurse behind the desk asks me delicately. She's being intentionally gentle with me, I can tell. Between the heat and the jet lag and the fear of the unknown, I must look, well... let's just say fragile. So the nurse speaks soothingly, and smiles a lot. She is arrestingly beautiful, with a movie star smile. There's a reason she is working the front desk. Behind her, a framed picture of Oprah beams out at me like a friend, reassuring me. I'm with people who have been Oprah-approved. How could anything go wrong?

"My name is Adrienne Arieff," I say, trying to sound breezy but failing miserably. I sound like I'm having an asthma attack. "I have an eleven-o'clock appointment."

"Dr. Patel will be with you shortly," the nurse says, then points me toward the waiting area, which consists of a collection of uncomfortable-looking institutional plastic chairs. By the looks of the other patients, slumped into their seats like they've been sitting there for hours and something somewhere is cramping up as a result, I could be in for a very long morning. I choose the most forgiving-looking seat I can find close to the door and do my best to look relaxed and comfortable. The moment I sit down, my left leg immediately starts to go numb. I realize I have been spoiled by the comfy chairs in Western waiting rooms, but not even the locals look comfortable in these!

An hour later, and fortunately while I still have feeling in my right leg, I'm summoned into the doctor's office. Not knowing what to expect, and on the verge of finally meeting the woman whom I have chosen to change my life forever, I am feeling very nervous and vaguely nauseous, as if a million swallowtail butterflies are flapping their wings in my solar plexus. Up until this moment, this has all been just a possibility. Now, it's real. This is *really happening.* And it's happening *now.*

Not that I'm unprepared. I've done my due diligence. I've scoured the Internet, read every source I could find, requested materials, called agencies, and checked more than ten references. I've gone back and forth for months in my head and with my husband and with anybody who would listen about the pros and cons of entering a foreign gestational surrogacy program. Would I be exploiting women (or one woman) in another country who had fewer advantages than I did? Would people think that I was just some spoiled girl who didn't want to go through the trouble of pregnancy and so was hiring somebody else to do it for her? Would people think I did this just so I wouldn't get fat? How was I going to feel about another woman's being pregnant with my baby? And was Dr. Patel's clinic a reputable institution, or was this another shady operation that had been set up to profit from the rising demand for Indian surrogates before proper regulatory practices could be put in place to meet the flood of demand?

"Atreff, Dr. Patel will see you now," says a shy-looking nurse with long, shiny black hair, in a brilliant yellow sari.

When I realize she is talking to me, I stand up, and once I regain feeling in my left leg, I limp down the hallway after her. Much like the ubiquitous traffic in the streets, the nurses in the hallway flow around me in a pattern only they can recognize. I try not to look at the huge hypodermic needles in their hands. I'm ushered into an office, offered yet another chair that I can tell is going to hold a grudge, and the door closes. The office itself is gloomy, a narrow room with a computer at one end and an ultrasound machine behind a fraying living room curtain at the other. I almost expect the Wizard of Oz to peek out at me from behind the curtain, demanding to know why I've come.

Instead, a lovely, soft-spoken woman looks up at me and smiles. "Hello, Adrienne, I am Dr. Nayna Patel. Welcome to Akanksha Clinic."

Dr. Patel is seated behind an enormous desk piled high with files, all containing, I imagine, the life histories of couples just like Alex and me, all looking to her and the clinic for a chance to have the family they've always dreamed of. She's making notes in one of these folders as I sit down. On the wall behind her is a diploma from Singapore University and yet another photograph of a radiant, reassuring Oprah, this time surrounded by jubilant couples, glowing surrogates, and happy, healthy babies.

I smile and begin to say something trivial and friendly to break the ice, but I'm interrupted by a nurse who comes through the door suddenly and whispers something in Dr. Patel's ear. As they discuss something in Gujarati that I can't understand, I notice that Dr. Patel looks much younger than her fifty-two years—I would have guessed a decade younger—with a warm, lovely face and a gentle, almost enigmatic, smile. I recognize her expression—passionate commitment tinged with utter exhaustion. Their press has been accurate; business at Akanksha is brisk.

"I'm very sorry to hear about your difficulties having a child," Dr. Patel says, dismissing the nurse, along with the years of heartbreak and frustration I have endured with a quick turn of the page. "As you know, I accept only patients, like yourself, who have an established infertility problem, so you have come to the right place. So let's see where we are today and whether or not we can make a start. I'll need you to have some blood taken, and then we'll do a sonogram, and then hopefully we can begin the IVF shots right away."

I immediately flash on the nurses with the large hypodermics.

"Could I . . . maybe have a glass of water?" Suddenly I find it difficult to swallow and my mouth feels like it's stuffed with cotton.

"Of course," Dr. Patel says, and motions to one of her staff. Her world moves quickly. There is a six-month waiting list at the clinic, and the list grows every day. There is little time to waste, and many new families to care for besides mine.

Two hours, three vials of blood, and a sonogram later, I am back in front of Dr. Patel, who is eyeing my results disapprovingly. I've seen that look so many times before, on the faces of other doctors, at other fertility clinics. I don't think I can bear to hear of another bad test result or live through another disappointment. I immediately fight the urge to run for the door.

"Now," she says, turning and addressing me suddenly, looking right into my eyes to make sure she has my full attention, "I will explain the process here at the clinic so we are clear, all right? As you know, we put you on birth control pills so that your period would be regulated. You should have stopped taking the pills three days ago, so you will start your period now. On the second day of your period, you will come back here, we will do some blood tests and an ultrasound, and if everything looks good, we will begin the fertility treatment. You will be coming here to the clinic once a day at ten a.m. for your treatment. You will be receiving one shot of Lupron and one shot of Zoladex, which are fertility drugs, to stimulate your overies."

Two shots, every day? No wonder there are so many women with hypodermic needles wandering around here.

"This cycle of the treatment will continue for ten days. You should expect to spend about an hour here at the clinic for each treatment. Periodically, we will be doing ultrasound tests to make sure that you are developing follicles. On the tenth day, we will do our final round of fertility drugs, and one last ultrasound. Then on day eleven you will have an HCG injection, the pregnancy hormone progesterone, which the body normally produces when conception occurs. This shot will encourage your eggs to mature. We will give you the shot at midnight, and then, thirty-six hours later, you will come here for your egg retrieval. You will be given medicine from an anesthesiologist so you will feel no pain during this process. You should plan on staying here at the clinic for a few hours after the procedure because you may feel a bit of cramping. We hope to retrieve anywhere from two to fifteen eggs, depending upon how many eggs you have produced.

"Your husband should plan on being here within twenty-four hours of the retrieval to provide a sperm sample. The lab will then fertilize the eggs that were retrieved, and three to five days after retrieval, three to five fertilized eggs will be transferred into your surrogate through a thin tube that is passed through the cervix. There is no pain associated with this procedure. Then, the surrogate will be placed on progesterone, and in two weeks, we will do a pregnancy test to see if the IVF has been successful. Do you have any questions about this process?"

I shook my head no, because I had so many questions that there was nothing to ask. She had just thrown so much information at me, information that I had read many times before, and yet now, on the verge of this all becoming real, it all sounded completely new, and terrifying.

"Well, I'm sure questions will arise as we move through, so please don't ever hesitate to talk to me if you are unclear about something. So, shall we get started?" Dr. Patel smiled and I felt instantly warmed and nodded my head yes. "Very good. When did you stop taking your birth control pill?"

"Umm, I didn't?" I said.

"Why did you not follow my directions?" Dr. Patel scolds. Then she looks at me, and simply waits. This is not a rhetorical question. Dr. Patel's face is impassive and stony; everything about her countenance says that she does not appreciate wasting her time with American slackers like me. Of course I don't have a good excuse. *How could I pack my bags, and hop on a plane to come to a fertility clinic for IVF treatment and forget to stop taking my birth control pills? Stupid. Stupid. Stupid!* Should I say I forgot? I misunderstood? Jet lag?

"I'm sorry," I say, deciding the best course is to fess up. "It was stupid. I don't know what I was thinking." Dr. Patel's face softens, and I think I even see a hint of a smile. The unvarnished truth was the right approach with Dr. Patel. After years of playing dodgeball with doctors and the cold hard facts, it is kind of a relief.

"Well," she says, ready to move things along. "I want you to go back to your hotel and relax." (Clearly, she is not familiar with my hotel.) "And go off your pill. On the second day of your next period, you come back and we'll begin."

"I'm so sorry . . . it's just so much to absorb. . . ." I begin to stammer, but Dr. Patel has already returned to the mountain of paper on her desk. We are done. This silence, I will come to understand later, is a good thing. Indians don't see a need to communicate further unless something is wrong. Satisfaction is generally met with silence. This is a huge personal and cultural adjustment for an American extrovert like me. I stand up and do what I'm told. Abhi meets me in the waiting room, takes one look at me, and leads me back out the door, laughing as usual with his arm around my shoulder.

On the way back to the hotel, I do feel an authentic sense of relief. The mystery is over, I'm no longer facing the unknown. My future has a face and I'm glad its Dr. Patel's. The clinic, once inside, is clean, efficient, and inviting; the staff is friendly. Dr. Patel, while not exactly long on bedside manner, is well-intentioned, talented, kind, and obviously in demand. And there is an air of acceptance about infertility and surrogacy as a whole at the Akanksha Infertility Clinic that I've found hard to come by at home. I know that I'm in excellent, understanding hands. But I have to confess to feeling something a little like disappointment. Another two days in a holding pattern under a mosquito net in my stiflingly hot hotel room is definitely not on the short list of my expectations. I feel inexplicably blue when I should be feeling exhilarated, and I am not sure why. I wish my husband, Alex, were here with me. He hadn't been able to get the time off work to come with me. He will be flying in when it's time to fertilize the eggs, but until then I am on my own.

At the time we planned this trip, I hadn't minded coming

alone. I'm a very independent spirit. As a general rule, I prefer to encounter my destiny solo, and one of the reasons that I love Alex is that he understands this about me and doesn't take offense. We need at least one of us at home earning money. This process isn't cheap, and the Akanksha Clinic doesn't take credit cards. We both agreed that I would go first, alone. But today I'm wondering about the wisdom of our choice. Today I really wish that my husband were here.

"India is very different than your country?" Abhi asks gently. It occurs to me that Abhi might be a more sensitive soul than I gave him credit for initially. He is once again sensing my discomfort and trying to distract me.

"You can say that again," I say. I see a patch of bright red geraniums blooming outside a mud hut. They are an invigorating splash of exuberance against the dun monotony of the baked dirt road. They remind me of my mother. I wish I could call her right now.

"America, it's very different than India, yes?" Abhi says again. He has taken me literally, which I find endearing.

"Yes, definitely different than San Francisco, where I live." I am trying to keep things as simple, light, and superficial as I can. But Abhi knows how to read between the lines.

"Ches, all the people feel this way first. But then, India puts its arms around chu and it starts to feel like home. Then, chu see, India is not so different. Well, hotter maybe. And more people."

"And more cows," I say.

"Ches, lotsa holy cows!" Abhi says with his laugh, which I realize is quite wonderful.

"Are you comfortable at the hotel?" Abhi asks me, and I can see he already knows the answer.

"Not really. The air-conditioning doesn't work," I say, feeling suddenly a little embarrassed. I don't want to be a poor sport, but one thought of that claustrophobic economy suite is enough to put me into a pout. I start to feel very sorry for myself all of a sudden. I am on my way back to an intolerably humid hotel room on the other side of the world while my husband is at home, probably eating a juicy steak and watching cable TV. I had to come all this way, on my own, to do what other people do without even thinking about it or, sometimes, even intend, ing to. I have to face skeptical friends, and negotiate a moun, tain of ethical and cross-cultural conundrums just to have a baby, while other women get to stay at home, rooted in the comfort and familiarity of their own lives, supported by friends and family, and eat ice cream and pickles. They get to feel that new life grow inside them, and even now, after all Alex and I have been through, I would still give anything to deal with a sore back and stretch marks. Instead I have to travel thousands of miles to sleep under a mosquito net for two days before the process can even begin.

"After your next appointment, we will move you to a new hotel, closer to the clinic. This is where the other clinic families are staying from all over the world. Chu will feel more com, fortable there. Chu will have good company."

I perk up. The thought of going to a new hotel is good enough news in itself, but the idea that I'll soon be able to meet and talk with other families embarking on the same journey that I am taking makes me feel a little better about things. This is an ad, venture, remember? And now I am going to meet my fellow travelers, some of whom probably know a lot more about the ter, rain than I do. This is a positive development indeed!

"Chu will see," says Abhi with a sweep of his hand that seems to take in the whole universe. "Wherever you go, the important things—they stay the same."

I could hug him. With a few simple words and another gesture that I don't quite fathom, Abhi has once again parted
the seas. My self-pity subsides. I'm so relaxed and optimistic
now that I'm not even troubled by the fact that Abhi is looking
directly into my eyes, instead of at the road ahead, and that
neither hand is on the wheel.

Speeding down an unmarked lane in a questionably main-
tained car with a kind and philosophical driver who definitely
does not have his eyes on the road is a strange place to discover
the quiet confidence that I have been lacking. But I have, I remind myself, always been at my best when in motion. As I look
out the window, for the first time I am filled with wonder and
appreciation for the stark and staggering beauty of the Indian
landscape. And I also begin to see the unusual beauty of my own
journey, which began with a desire to finally put down roots, and
would lead me thousands of miles from home in order to plant
the seeds.

chapter 3

I've been a hopeless romantic since I was about twelve, and by my early twenties, I had learned, most times the hard way, that it's better to enter into romance cautiously, rationally, *slowly*, rather than rush in only to have your hopes dashed and your heart broken.

My first love was an African-American boy named Scott Johnson. Scott was a mature fourteen years old to my youthful twelve. He was charming and wonderful, and I was besotted. But Scott left me for Mary, who, at just eleven years old, was already six feet tall and looked like a supermodel. I was only twelve and had already been dumped for a younger woman! I was outraged by the injustice.

High school and college were filled with crushes and short-lived relationships, but no one boy caught my heart. After college, I moved to New York to start my career in public relations, eager for love to find me. Then, one night, I went to a dinner party and fell head over heels in love at first sight with Javier from Chile. We actually only met face-to-face that one enchanted evening, and then he went back to Chile while I stayed in New York. For over a year, Javier and I wrote passionate letters to each other, purple with emotion and unfulfilled longing. At the ripe old age of twenty-six, my whole life had changed. I didn't do any of the things my girlfriends were doing that year:

dating and partying. Instead I worked, went to the gym, and at night I poured my heart into those letters to Javier. I was completely absorbed with my pen pal. He would leave phone messages that said things like "My mind and heart are in the clouds dreaming of you. I can't do anything except think of you." How could I resist?

Finally Javier bought me a ticket to come and visit him in Chile for two weeks. We had an amazing time together, but we quickly realized that our relationship was rooted in a fantasy—I couldn't start my career from Chile and he wasn't moving to New York. We couldn't spend the rest of our love lives in letters. So, although our hearts were breaking, we went our separate ways after those two weeks.

I was grief-stricken. My relationship with Javier had taken over my life, to the exclusion of all other things. But though I was sad and depressed following our breakup, I also felt more mature, more of a woman, after that relationship ended. I had learned that I could make a decision that was in my best interests, even if it was a tough one.

Just as before, I worked and went to the gym, but in the long, lonely evenings, there was no one to pour my heart out to—not even on the page. Loving Javier had made me realize that I could fall deeply and passionately in love just through the intimacy of letters. I went on dates, and there were a string of forgettable romances after Javier. There was Gordon the diamond heir and Robert the tech entrepreneur. I moved to London and, burning the candle at both ends, traveled extensively for work while in my down time I was trying to have a little fun. I wasn't looking for anything serious. And then Alex came along and changed all that.

❋ ❧❋❧ ❋

I met Alex through a mutual friend, Chelsea. She invited both of us on a New Year's trip to Cabo San Lucas. Alex had booked a slot for himself and the girlfriend he hadn't met yet, months earlier. He was confident that by the time New Year's rolled around, he would have found someone to share Cabo with. However, things didn't work out quite as he had planned, so, to help Alex out of an extra expense, the slot was offered to me. And I took it.

The six of us met at the gate to board our flight for Cabo. I was dressed for a cold winter's day in San Francisco, even though it was temperate in California and we were headed to Mexico (I've always defied trend). Alex was forewarned, sartorially speaking, of what he was getting into right from the beginning. Alex was a new partner at a litigation law firm, so he had spent the last couple of years with his head down, working long hours at the office at the expense of just about everything in his life except accrued vacation days and frequent flyer miles (to this day, Alex often teases me that were it not for his six-figure frequent flyer account, we never would have gotten off the ground as a couple).

We hit it off immediately. Alex was kind, smart, and could make me laugh. He was the sort of man I wanted to stay friends with even after I got back from Mexico.

I returned to my busy London life, but we stayed in touch. Several months later, I was back in California, and my friends put together a dinner at a neighborhood restaurant in San Francisco. At the last minute, I decided to invite Alex. I wanted to make plans with him, and I thought a group setting would make things more easy and relaxed. So, there we were at this restaurant, talking non-stop and laughing the entire night together. Two of my close friends noticed the chemistry; they

said that Alex was the perfect guy for me and I should stop dat,
ing jerks and take a serious look at this hot guy, who just hap,
pened to be a nice guy, too. Before I knew it, Alex and I were
seeing each other every night, and my friends, who seemed to
know what was good for me better than I did, encouraged me to
keep seeing him.

When I went back to London, Alex and I started emailing
all the time. Email, I discovered, was much more satisfying
than the long love letters I had sent to Javier, because it was
more immediate. But that relationship had taught me the im,
portance of actually seeing each other on a regular basis. Alex
agreed to meet me in Venice for the weekend, and then, just
two weeks later, he was my date at a friend's wedding in the
hills of Portugal. I began to realize that here was a man who
was willing to step way out of his comfort zone in order to
meet me (quite literally) more than halfway. After that week,
end in Portugal, we weren't just casually dating anymore. We
weren't quite ready to take the next step—weren't even sure
what that step was—but we knew we wanted to be together.

After eight months of emails, long,distance phone calls, and
romantic getaways, Alex's frequent flyer account edged into
the red just as my high,profile dot,com company in London
lost funding and closed its doors. I needed to go home to San
Francisco to regroup and rethink my career. Alex, completely
out of the blue, asked me to move in with him. And I, the
world traveler who didn't think she could settle down, said
yes.

When I fell in love with Alex, something changed in me. Alex
made me feel peaceful and in control. He was the calm intellec,
tual that I was not. Alex was stable and careful where I was im,
pulsive and uncensored. We were the perfect pair of opposites.
Of course Alex was the next step. I had known it all along.

Our wedding took place during the one, all-too-brief, remission my mom snatched from cancer. It lasted only a few weeks, but for that very short time, my mom and I had the gift of worrying about things like the color of the tablecloths at the head table or if I should wear wedges or heels, and shopping for everything under the sun. It was wonderful. But by the time I got home from my honeymoon, the cancer had returned, more voracious and fierce than ever.

Alex and I never really had the chance to be giddy, carefree newlyweds, because I spent the first few years of our marriage taking care of my mother. Alex never once complained. My friends were right. He was the kind of guy who was going to really be there for me and stick around.

✻❃✻❃✻

They say first comes love, then comes marriage. Well, I'd done those things with joy, but I wasn't so sure about Adrienne and Alex with the baby carriage. Motherhood had never really been in my master plan. My life felt complete already. I was thirty-three, and I owned my own business, which required me to divide my time between my offices in San Francisco and New York. In short, I was really busy and happy, and so was Alex. But something was missing for both of us, though neither of us could articulate what it was.

And then my friend Alexandra had a baby. From the moment I held her new daughter in my arms, I felt an instant connection. I realized, to my utter amazement, that I really was ready to become a mother myself. This was a bit unexpected, and a little hard to wrap my head around at first. Alex and I were both busy professionals, with full work lives and personal commitments. How would we fit a baby into that lifestyle? Whether or not we would have a child had been one of those hypothetical questions that existed in the far distant future, to be answered someday, but now, that someday was here!

And I must confess that, just as with love, I was afraid of disappointment. I don't feel comfortable wanting anything too badly—it's like putting my emotions onstage for everyone to view. I always try to protect myself from getting hurt, so I err on the side of caution. I think I do this because both my parents were so independent that even as a kid, I was encouraged and became comfortable doing my own thing. The thought of relying on people made me feel anxious, so even at an early age, I was more independent than most. But, becoming parents and sharing that experience was something that both Alex and I knew that we wanted, so, at thirty-three years old, I was ready to embark on my biggest endeavor yet: getting pregnant and becoming a mother.

❀❀❀❀❀

Like most women, I started with a routine appointment with my OB/GYN. I was actually *excited* as I sat in the waiting room, if you can imagine such a thing. You know you're a little giddy when stirrups and a speculum don't set you back. I've never liked going to the doctor, but in that moment, I was on top of the world.

The doctor asked normal questions. I gave normal answers. I mentioned some lower abdominal pain. She just shrugged and told me to watch the late-night snacks and call her if things got worse. She didn't seem worried, so I didn't worry either. I hadn't anticipated that there would be any difficulties. I was a healthy thirty-three-year-old with a gym membership and a pretty respectable BMI. My mother had gotten pregnant easily and quickly. "All systems are go," said my doctor, smiling routinely. "Don't drink, and have fun."

I followed the doctor's orders to the letter. Well, it's not like they were that hard. I had fun and purposeful sex with my adorable husband as often as I could, and sure enough, I was pregnant one month later. It had all been so easy. I started eating pasta for two, and my husband and I began to prepare for our baby-to-be. I must have driven my friends crazy—I couldn't pass a baby store without oohing and aahing at the miniature furniture and clothes. My more seasoned friends smiled and tried to look patient. Alex was predictably amazing—coming home with ideas for names, bringing me anything he thought I would enjoy. I was in heaven.

And then, everything changed. Those abdominal cramps I had told my doctor about at my checkup got worse. Alex told me that I should go to the doctor, just to reassure myself that it was nothing. I made an appointment, and after a thorough exam, I discovered that those lower abdominal cramps didn't have *anything* to do with late-night ice cream. My doctor had been wrong, terribly wrong. Everything *wasn't* normal. I had uterine fibroids the size of grapefruits.

When I told Alex the news he paused for a moment, as if deciding how to feel, and then said simply, "We're getting the best doctor we can find, and everything is going to be okay." My mother had always taught me not to focus on the mountain peak but instead to focus on the next ledge, and pull myself up, one handhold at a time. It makes keeping a positive outlook much, much easier, and apparently, Alex had also learned this technique.

I found myself in the care of the best high-risk pregnancy specialist in town, and happily entered my twentieth week of pregnancy looking and feeling fantastic. I had great skin, shiny hair, and tons of energy. Gone were my earlier fears and now, under the watchful eye of my doctor's expert care, I was once again filled with hope for the pregnancy and the excitement of a baby on the way. I was in a state of perpetual retail ecstasy, shopping the mommy traps all over town to get ready. I didn't want to have a shower before the birth because in the Jewish religion you wait until after the birth, but that didn't stop my impatient friends from sending me gifts. Alex and I chose to have genetic testing done; we learned that we were having a healthy baby girl, and we named our daughter Colette.

Alex and I did nothing but gab endlessly about how gorgeous Colette was, how she already looked so beautiful from the sonogram pictures. She looked so happy and moved so freely while we watched her on the screen. She was fully formed and weighed around two and a half pounds. Alex and I fell in love with her instantly.

Never in my life had things felt better. I could see on the sonogram right in front of me that Colette was perfect. Everything was perfect. My fears of disappointment completely vanished. What could go wrong if I was feeling this right? With my doctor's blessing, Alex and I decided to take a quick vacation to relax and enjoy each other before Colette was born and our lives changed forever. We picked a destination close to home—Malibu, the chill-and-grill capital of the world. Alex and I drove down the coast with our dog, Zoe, in tow, and settled into our favorite little place on the ocean. Life felt blissful, easy, alive with excitement. I was filled with joyful anticipation about what would come.

On the last day, Alex, Zoe, and I took a long, brisk walk on the beach. It was a gorgeous Malibu morning, with just a whisper of a breeze off the water. I could see Catalina perfectly. *See, there is a God,* I thought, taking in the natural splendor. In that moment, everything felt divinely ordained.

But by the time we'd returned to the hotel, my mood had shifted. Instead of joy and enthusiastic expectation, I was filled with an intense and instantaneous sense of foreboding. Something was wrong.

The next minute, as I stood in the kitchenette, my water broke. Then I began to bleed. This was not the light spotting that many women recognize as a fairly common and benign part of pregnancy. I was *covered* with blood, as if someone had shot me. It felt like horrific cramps but worse. I was terrified and shocked this was happening. I looked up at my husband, and I could tell he didn't have the first idea what to do. Alex simply froze. This scared me even more, so I frantically called my father. Somehow, through my hysterical tears, I was able to tell him what was happening to me. I needed help. I had to save my baby. My father, calm and collected in crisis, told me to get to Cedars-Sinai in Beverly Hills as soon as possible. He was on staff at the hospital and he would meet me there.

The one-hour drive from Malibu to Beverly Hills felt interminable. When we finally got to the hospital, I was admitted immediately and rushed into an exam room. A nurse hurriedly squirted gel on my stomach, running the sonogram wand in circles in a desperate search for a heartbeat. I held my breath. Colette came into view, perfect and so fragile—and still. I held my breath. There was no heartbeat. Colette had died.

My fibroids had grown so large that they had forced premature labor. I had had a stillbirth at twenty weeks. When they told us that there was no saving our child, I just wanted to die in that hospital, like my baby had. I wasn't strong. I was angry and alone in my grief.

I simply couldn't believe that this had happened. Everyone knows that the first trimester is the most dangerous, but I was nearly in my third trimester and feeling great. I had been reassured over and over again by my doctor that the baby was developing normally, with no sign of imminent danger. It never occurred to me that, again, my doctor could be wrong. Looking back, I realize that I had an almost childlike belief in medical technology, I hadn't doubted my doctor for one second. But I know it's a bit more complex than that. Medical science can't guarantee anything 100 percent, and certainly, there are no sure things in life no matter how good your specialist is. Alex and I both knew that our pregnancy was high-risk, but we focused on the positive, and each good report from a test or sonogram confirmed every hope and outdistanced every fear. If there was only a 10 percent chance of success, we focused on the 10 percent and denied every other possibility. Our doctor wanted the best for us as well and worked so hard for a good outcome for all of us. He hadn't been able to prepare me for this event, and he didn't have the information to help me deal with it emotionally once it happened.

Leaving the hospital and getting back to San Francisco remains a blur. I spent the next three months feeling like hell. I fluctuated between feeling completely numb and totally hypersensitive. I could be cold and detached one moment, and burst into ragged, wild tears the next. I started to miss meetings at work and would sometimes drink a bottle of wine on my own. Alex and I didn't talk much. We ate a lot of sushi and drank a lot of sake. I cried a lot. We watched TV and cheesy comedies, though I was more drawn to dark, depressing dramas like *The Diving Bell and the Butterfly* and *Life Is a House*, films that matched my gloom.

I became myopically fixated on who was checking in on me via email and phone—I think I was desperate for my friends and family, and some really rose to the occasion and made me feel so loved during such a terrible time. My friend Matthew would call weekly, leaving a nice short message saying he was thinking of me. Other friends were Michelle and Nicole, who would always check in, asking me to do something, and Sasha, who sent notes and text messages filled with X's and O's. My sister, Allison, would buy me groceries and give me books she had just read—she always had great taste in books. These little check-ins, these small actions to remind me that there were people who loved me and wanted to support me and Alex through this disaster, made a world of difference.

Most of my friends were amazing. But my pregnant friends tended to steer clear of me. It was as if there was something wrong with me, and whatever it was, it might be contagious. For expectant moms, I was their worst nightmare.

After those first few terrible weeks, I tried to tell myself that I was fine. I started going out again, mostly to work functions here and there. I had gained quite a bit of weight from the pregnancy—double portions of pasta and pizza during those first queasy weeks—and now, after the loss, I was overindulging in sugary foods and alcoholic drinks and never venturing outside for a walk or a run to get exercise and fresh air. After a friend's wedding, I remember looking at photos and wondering who had invited the chubby, unhappy woman. I had to do a double take; the miserable woman was me. I literally didn't recognize myself. I had always been fit and lean and now I saw that I looked heavy and aged. It was time to make a change.

I started small. I put money away in a retirement plan, took up yoga again, and decided I was my own best friend, so I had to treat myself well. I went on adventures in an attempt to cleanse myself, body, mind and spirit. I traveled to China, Morocco, the Caribbean, London, Argentina, Mexico, Hawaii, Madrid, and Venezuela. Alex would meet me for long weekends all over the world; we were finally talking to each other the way we had before we lost Colette. Fortunately, he had built back his frequent flyer account by then, because we were hitting it hard. I needed to be on the move—sitting gave me too much time to think—and as I traveled across continents and over oceans, I started to develop an inner strength that I had never known before.

The miscarriage was so awful, it broke me in ways that I will never be able to articulate or ever fully heal from. But I learned to endure the unendurable. I didn't feel like my old self, but I started to feel like a woman I recognized, and a woman I was proud to be.

Then, during a weekend with dear friends in Tuscany, I took a pregnancy test and discovered that I was pregnant again. I was with Alex and my three surrogate sisters, Sasha, Sora, and Alexandra. It was an unexpected, magical moment. Once again, I was filled with the exhilaration of a coming baby. We celebrated with bubbly water for me and champagne for everyone else. After the fire, bliss had returned.

When we got back from Italy, I went to my doctor for my first sonogram. Based on my own calculations, I was already at fourteen weeks, so I had passed the first-trimester safety mark. I was filled with nervous excitement when I lay down on the examination table and the nurse ran the sensor over my belly. I looked expectantly at the screen. Nothing happened. All I saw was a black dot, and I knew what that meant—no heartbeat.

The nurse teared up and called for the doctor. My stomach clenched. It was all so terribly familiar, and yet I couldn't accept that this was happening again. How could this happen *again*? The doctor came in, looked at the sonogram and sighed. There was nothing to be done.

I had gone into the office with the sun literally shining over me and, as I left, dark clouds covering the sun and darkening the sky. Rain began to pour down, but I walked in puddles the three miles to Alex's office without even realizing it was rain-ing. I met him, soaked through and sobbing, at the Starbucks in his office building. He held me while I cried.

After my first miscarriage, my doctor told me that I should have a myomectomy to remove the uterine fibroids. I decided to go through with the surgery. I was in the hospital four days. The pain was excruciating, and the surgery left me with a scar that looked very much like a C-section scar right at the bottom of my abdomen.

After the surgery, I decided to get strong. I made up my mind that a successful pregnancy was within my control, and I was going to take charge. Unlike my first loss, I started to eat all the right foods. I exercised like a maniac and took prenatal vitamins religiously. I waited another three months to start trying again. When I felt ready—prepared and vigilant—I started to track my ovulation cycles with sticks that produced a happy face every time it was time to try to make another baby. I was in control—I was *ready* for the next pregnancy. This time, it wouldn't catch me by surprise.

Two months later, I took a pregnancy test and all my hard work had paid off. I was pregnant again! This time, though, as with love, I had learned to be cautious. I would take nothing for granted and would be *so* careful. I told no one, not even my husband. A few more weeks passed, and the day before my first doctor's appointment, I started to bleed. I had suffered a third miscarriage.

This loss was heartbreaking and no easier to come to terms with than the earlier two. I had made a promise to Alex and to myself that after three miscarriages, we would try a new approach. The toll of these losses on my spirit, my body, and my marriage was simply too damaging. Something had to change. It was time to find another way.

Alex and I started with a conversation with my doctor. My

doctor told me that I was a perfect candidate for surrogacy because I had had multiple miscarriages. I had always thought that surrogacy was for couples that had difficulty getting pregnant, but after talking with my doctor, I discovered that surrogacy was also a common path for couples who were able to conceive but were not able to maintain the pregnancy. Then Alex, ever the thorough researcher, found an article in the *New York Times* about surrogacy in India. I had never given surrogacy much thought, but the article intrigued me.

The story in the *Times* was about a fertility program run by a woman named Dr. Nayna Patel, who had recently been featured on *The Oprah Winfrey Show*. Her clinic was in a small town called Anand. Her program was unique in that it was a one-stop shop that took care of all the complexities involved with accomplishing a birth through surrogacy in one carefully monitored and safe location.

This sounded intriguing to both of us, so I looked up the Akanksha Infertility Clinic on the Web and learned whatever I could about Dr. Patel and her work. Akanksha was unique in many respects, I discovered. For one thing, they provided housing for the surrogates during the pregnancy, which was important not only for the health of the surrogates and of the babies that they were carrying, but also because in many small villages in India, surrogacy is frowned upon, and in some cases surrogates are the victims of violence.

❊❧❊❧❊

The surrogate house looked similar to a college dorm, with sparse rooms and everything tucked away neatly and carefully behind built-in cupboards. The beds were neatly aligned in an airy and pleasant room, with healthy, happy-looking young women scattered in small clusters throughout the room, all smiling, all in various stages of pregnancy. They were watched over by gentle, pleasant-looking nurses. It seemed overall like a happy, positive place to be, for everybody concerned. The advantages of the surrogate house were many, including a built-in support system. All medical services, meals, and classes, like a popular English course, were provided to ensure that the women were well cared for as well as intellectually and socially engaged. Husbands and children could visit freely.

The Akanksha website states that surrogates are carefully selected and must go through medical and psychological checks to ensure that they are physically and mentally up to the challenges of surrogacy. Only women who are already mothers can become surrogates. Once they are pregnant, surrogates are given weekly checkups and prenatal vitamins, and are nourished and cared for by clinic staff through the term of the pregnancy.

Alex and I were also comforted to learn that surrogate mothers are bound by contract to give the newborn to the biological parents immediately after delivery. This was encouraging, because in the United States, where the legal restrictions concerning surrogacy vary from state to state, such contracts requiring that the baby be given over to the intended parents are rarely enforceable. In cases of dispute, custody tends to be granted to the surrogate rather than to the biological parents. After so much disappointment, the idea that an American surrogate could change her mind at the last moment was terrifying.

Dr. Patel's contract further required that all fees are paid in cash installments, with the bulk of the fee being paid after the birth. We calculated that the cost of surrogacy at the Akanksha

Clinic would be about $25,000 to $35,000, roughly a third of the typical price in the United States. This included the cost of the medical procedures; payment to the surrogate mother, through the clinic; as well as travel to and from India.

In addition to surrogacy, the clinic also worked with patients who wanted to do just IVF—when eggs are harvested from the genetic mother and then implanted back in her own womb—as well as IUI (intrauterine insemination), the placement of sperm directly into the uterus. The most popular procedure was IVF (in vitro fertilization), in which the sperm and eggs are collected from the genetic parents and fertilized in the laboratory, and the resulting embryos are placed in the uterus of either the genetic mother herself or the waiting surrogate.

Everything that we had learned about Dr. Patel and her clinic appealed to Alex and me very much, but I had my doubts about going through such an intensive and uncertain process so far away from home—more than eight thousand miles, in fact. Undergoing surrogacy and medical procedures and having my baby be born abroad, all in a developing nation, was daunting. Even so, domestic surrogacy seemed even riskier to us because of the complex web of U.S. laws. All I had to do was think of the name *Mary Beth Whitehead** or of her daughter, known as Baby M, to give myself pause about going through this process domestically. It worked for a lot of people but it wasn't for me. I couldn't deal with any more disappointments.

---

* Iver Peterson, "Baby M's Future," *New York Times*, April 5, 1987. "Last week, in a decision that created law in the legislative vacuum surrounding surrogate mother-hood, Judge Harvey R. Sorkow of New Jersey Superior Court awarded custody of one-year-old Baby M to William Stern, the child's natural father, and his wife, Elizabeth. He stripped Mary Beth Whitehead, the mother, of all parental rights, and ruled that the contract she had signed with the Sterns was enforceable despite material misrepresentations by the Sterns."

After weeks of Web-surfing for every factoid I could find on foreign surrogacy, my pro and con list was still pretty evenly balanced. It was true that there were complicated issues surrounding some foreign surrogacy clinics—my primary question was always whether these women were being forced into surrogacy—and they brought up thorny ethical questions. I found advocates who said that being a surrogate mother, regardless of economic status, is a choice that enhances a woman's rights, while others argue that the practice is equivalent to prostitution. I myself did not feel we would be morally or physically compromising or exploiting anyone. A surrogate could earn the equivalent of five years' salary for just one surrogacy, which I thought would only change her and her whole family's life for the better, and as long as she was not coerced and chose to do it of her own free will, I was not arrogant enough to believe that I knew better.

I was fundamentally drawn to the idea of helping another woman and making a difference in her life, just as she was making such a tremendous difference in ours. But I worried about what other people would think. Was I going to seem like some snotty rich girl who was paying somebody in a developing world to carry my child because I didn't want to get fat? And, more significantly, could I stand behind my beliefs and feel good about my decision, no matter what anybody else had to say about it? Whenever I expressed these worries, Alex would roll his eyes. "Sure, Adrienne," he'd say, "that's what everybody who knows you is going to think. You're doing surrogacy in India because you don't want to bloat."

Alex was right. Everybody knew what we'd been through. The people who mattered would understand that I hadn't made this decision frivolously. For many women, miscarriages are private and occur so early in the pregnancy, they have not yet shared their happy news. But I had lost Colette well into my second trimester; even casual acquaintances and business colleagues knew of Alex's and my heartbreak. Surely nobody was going to begrudge us this chance for happiness. As I started to share the idea with my friends, it turned out I was right. Almost without exception, we found our friends to be supportive, and excited that we were embarking on a new plan. Everyone knew how hard we had tried and how badly we wanted a baby.

Everybody, that is, with one exception. When I told my dear friend Monica about our new plan, she gasped in horror. "You can't rent a womb from some poor woman in an underdeveloped nation," she said. "It's completely and utterly unethical." Unethical? Complicated, yes, but morally wrong? Monica's harsh words felt like a slap in the face.

"How could you ever live with yourself?"

Her quick and uncompromising judgment took me by surprise. I still had mixed emotions about the idea myself— Alex and I were by no means committed to this plan, simply exploring it and sharing our hopes with close friends—so I was unprepared for condemnation, especially from a friend whose sound judgment I was used to relying on. I had found the subject complicated and nuanced, but for Monica, it was as stark as black and white. There was no room for discussion or parsing out what made sense from what didn't. For her, it was right versus wrong. Was she wrong? Was I? Whatever Monica's position, I felt that she was being very judgmental, and intentionally cruel. I was surprised at the passion of her conviction, as she was someone who had never been in my position, and so was, in my view, really in no position to judge me.

And in that moment, I realized how I *truly* felt. For Alex and me, surrogacy in India was the right decision. As painful as it was to hear Monica's serious doubts, her questions and condemnation clarified my convictions.

Surrogacy advocates in the United States will tell you not to get involved with poor surrogates under any circumstances because it can lead to exploitation. I initially disagreed with this line of thinking. Charges of "renting a womb" and exploitation have long tarnished the practice of surrogacy. But in my mind, a woman going through the risks of labor for another family clearly deserves to be paid. To me, this was not exploitation. This was a win-win, allowing the surrogate to have a brighter future and the couple to have a child. If my money was going to benefit an Indian woman financially for a service she willingly provided, I preferred that it be a poor woman who really needed help because the money that a surrogate earns in India is, to be blunt, life-changing.

I wanted to be certain that the woman who helped me and Alex to become parents would be fully in charge of her decision; Dr. Patel assured me that this would be the case, and at that point, Alex and I agreed that we would write to Dr. Patel and ask her to begin looking for a surrogate for us.

It was a month before we had any word at all. Then, on a Thursday afternoon, while we were out at our favorite sushi joint, Alex and I received the news from Dr. Patel that our surrogate had been found.

"Her name is Vaina. She is twenty-six years old and speaks Hindi and the Gujarati languages," Dr. Patel had written. "We have an interpreter here so you two can communicate. Please get on a plane to India and arrive here before July 14 to begin treatment."

After losses, indecision, and heartbreak, the right road forward was suddenly so clear and right before me. And all I had to do was get on a plane.

chapter 4

"Good morning, Atren, now we go to the clinic," says Abhi, who bursts into my hotel room like a sunbeam through haze. He begins gathering up my things to move them to the new hotel. Abhi has friends virtually everywhere in Anand, and the owner of the Hotel Laksh must be high on the list. Most of the couples who come to Akanksha stay there. Abhi turns and tries to conjure me out of the bed by waving his hands. "We must not be late for the clinic," he says. I remember that arched eyebrow of Dr. Patel's and hop out of bed.

Abhi leads me downstairs and up to a remarkably well-appointed rickshaw. Apparently, Abhi is a man of many vehicles.

"Air-conditioning?" I ask, already wilting in the morning sun.

"No," says Abhi regretfully, "but it is a very good rickshaw." He helps me into my seat, which sways and groans as I climb in. "I'll go fast, so lotsa breeze. No problem!"

He's wrong about the breeze. He's wrong about the fast part too. It's morning rush hour and it's a laborious journey of hurry up and wait. But I have to admit that there's something very romantic about a rickshaw. I feel more vitally connected to the life in the streets. I can almost reach out and touch the cows and the elephants and the people as we pass. I can smell the incense and the rich foods simmering in the roadside vendor carts, hear the barking and the honking and the fireworks exploding. I can feel India.

Anand is not on any tourist maps. There aren't any historical landmarks here, no masterpieces of ancient architecture, no four-star restaurants. There are no movie posters advertising the latest Holly- or Bollywood blockbuster, for there are no movie theaters, no Western shops, no chain stores. It isn't memorable.

Yet it's beautiful, in an honest way. The streets are filled with women and children—I've never seen so many beautiful women—and there is always the smell of incense in the air. The women dress in colors as bold and vibrant as a Frank Stella painting. There seem to be flowers and lit candles everywhere, and the harmony of chanting rises from every tiny alley, welcoming me to this new world.

❀ ✿❀✿ ❀

Abhi makes the turn onto Station Road, barely missing a scooter carrying three people, and pulls up to the clinic. I've arrived, and in one piece. The family of beggars that sat outside the gates my first visit has been replaced by a new and larger one. The cows don't seem to have moved an inch.

Inside, single women and couples sit in the same plastic chairs, looking just as uncomfortable as the last batch. I join them, and everyone looks up at me and smiles sympathetically as I choose my chair. Within minutes I'm called in to Dr. Patel's office. She is sitting in the same place I left her, once again dressed in a richly colored sari that makes her look like medical royalty. She flips through my file with a detached efficiency. I almost feel the urge to curtsy.

"Have a seat, Adrienne," she says, examining my sonogram closely as I try to get a peek around the desk to catch a glimpse.

The blue light from her computer monitor seems to be her primary focus, so I am trying my best to act casual, but I really want to look at the computer screen with her. I choose to exercise restraint, and wait for her. She finally turns her attention to me with a pleased look.

"So, we will begin your treatment today," she says, looking very satisfied. I release a huge sigh of relief. "We will do your first shots today and then two shots every day for two weeks, okay? And then, with any luck at all, we will be ready for harvest and fertilization. Do you have any questions you wish to ask me?"

Questions. Yes, questions. What do I want to know? What do I *not* want to know? Before I can put a verb and a noun together, two of those efficient, unflappable nurses with needles in their hands enter and one of them, gently but completely without warning, administers my first shot in the arm. Ouch! I stand, trying not to be a baby about it, but that was more than the innocent pinch of a tetanus shot. I take a few deep breaths to steady myself. I lean slightly over the back of my chair, and when I do, I get a second and bigger shot on the left side of my bum.

"Ummm. Ouch!" I say, starting to feel a tad woozy as the hormones rush into my system.

Seated outside the office and watching the proceedings, four women flinch, regarding me with large, startled eyes. They know they're next. Things move so slowly around here, and then suddenly, they are upon you in an instant. India always manages to catch me off guard.

Before I leave to get my blood drawn, Dr. Patel says casually, "Oh, Adrienne, I have arranged a meeting for you with your surrogate in an hour. Are you ready to meet her?" This stops me in my tracks, and I don't feel the sore spot from the needle anymore. It has been replaced by sheer terror.

"You mean in an hour, like, an hour from *now*?"

"Yes, today! She is a very good and faithful girl. She is Gujarati, and very dedicated to the surrogacy. A very, very nice girl," says Dr. Patel, closing my file.

I nod, give a slight, terrified smile, and wander through the clinic halls to find a chair until my surrogate arrives. An hour cannot pass quickly enough, and yet I am dreading its end. Once again I'm living one second at a time, and each one of those seconds contains a question: How am I going to feel meeting the woman who is going to carry my child? What will I say? Will she understand me? How will she feel meeting me?

I have no frame of reference for an experience like this, and no idea of what to expect. Maybe some fresh air will help. Anything is better than sitting in these chairs. I walk through the dirt roads surrounding the clinic, deciding to just get lost in the overwhelming atmosphere of village life. I find it comforting to be distracted by a place so completely foreign to me. I can forget the rising din of my inner thoughts and instead focus on what is going on right in front of me, namely, avoiding the motor vehicles zigzagging around me and finding someplace where I can get a bottle of water and something salty to eat. I buy some almonds and, remarkably, Poland Spring water, though I am worlds away from Maine. I glance at my watch and realize that almost an hour has passed. I better get back to the clinic in a hurry or I'll be late for the most important meeting of my life.

I hail a rickshaw, which sputters and whines its way to a halt and idles plaintively, bursting black clouds of smoke that hover in the still, moist air. I hand the driver a piece of paper with the clinic's address on it and somehow make it back with seconds to spare. The traffic gods have been kind to me.

"Hello, I'm Ayisha," says a slight but strong-looking woman with bright, penetrating eyes and a long black braid down her back at the entrance. "I'm the translator here at the Akanksha Clinic. I'll be with you in your meeting today with your surrogate, Vaina. Will you come with me, please?"

"Thank you so much," I say, and follow Ayisha down the hall to a small office at the back of the clinic with many plastic chairs and an old wooden desk from the 1950s. And there, in the corner of the room, she sits. She looks shy and sweet, and has long hair that shines from good health and plenty of oil. Her large, liquid eyes sparkle like twilight on deep, still water. After an initial glance, she lowers her eyes and stares at her hands, which are resting uneasily in her lap.

"I'm so happy to meet you. My name is Adrienne Arieff. What is your name?" My voice sounds high-pitched and forced. I'm trying too hard. I realize instantly that this is a mistake, but I'm so nervous I can't help it. The translator repeats what I've said, and Vaina smiles but still doesn't look at me. She whispers something to the translator, who tells me that she is happy to meet me too.

I sit down across from her and gently take her hand, trying to stop myself from assaulting her with a barrage of questions, but I want to ask her how she is feeling about her choice. I want to know if she is being pressured into this decision in any way, I want to know what her life is like with her husband and children at home in her village. I want to know how they feel about this decision.

Women don't have it easy in India. It gets a little better every day, as more and more women become educated and achieve economic independence, but these advantages are not for women from small villages like Vaina. A crime against women is committed every three minutes in India.[1] India has what Nicholas Kristoff[2] (my hero of writers) would refer to as a "modern slave" class—millions of women and girls in brothels, held prisoner with no future.[3] Of children between the ages of seven and fourteen who are not enrolled in school, 55 percent are girls, as girls represent just 48 percent of all seven- to fourteen-year-old children in India.[4]

With all of my fears about this process and about the horrific statistics on women and exploitation in the country, my biggest priority was that Vaina had not been forced or pressured into doing this. I wanted to be sure that this decision was her own, and that she feels safe and happy about her decision to become our surrogate. Dr. Patel assured me from the beginning that she only accepts surrogates who come to the clinic of their own free will, but given some of these women's circumstances, what does "free will" really mean? Nearly all surrogates do so in order to benefit their own families. And I am aware of the gravity of the stigma attached to Indian surrogates when they return to their home villages. In many villages, surrogacy is considered adultery, the worst act a woman can commit. Most would lose everything if they were discovered.

Vaina looks as nervous as I feel, which makes me feel an instant kinship with her. We are traveling down the same road together, at least in this moment, and neither one of us appears to have a clue about where we are headed. I wish she would look at me rather than at her clasped hands. This will never work if Vaina and I cannot treat each other with respect, candor, and compassion. We must regard each other as equals.

"We are so grateful for what you are doing for us," I say. It's very important to me that she understand how much her generous act means to Alex and me. Meeting Vaina and seeing her face-to-face, I feel in a distinct and powerful way how grateful I am for having found her and for the gift she is giving to my husband and me. The translator explains what I've said, and

Vaina looks a little embarrassed and doesn't seem to know how to respond. I think I may have slammed into a cultural wall without realizing it.

"I've brought you a present," I say, trying to switch gears and introduce a little levity into the weighty atmosphere.

"Thank you," Vaina says, accepting the present I have brought her, a box of Ghirardelli chocolates from San Francisco. She opens it politely. I am touched by her use of English, but she still seems very withdrawn. I'm not sure what I was hoping for—an embrace, instant intimacy, girl talk—but whatever it was, it isn't happening. Not even chocolate is bringing her out of her shell.

"How many children do you have?" I ask.

Vaina holds up three fingers.

"Girls or boys?" I ask. She tells me she has four-year-old twin boys and one seven-year-old daughter. When Vaina speaks about her family, her eyes light up. I don't understand the words she's saying, but I can hear the love and pride. I give her the M&M's I brought for her children, and the atmosphere in the room warms instantly.

It's customary to bring or send presents to your surrogate, like clothes for their kids from brands like Old Navy and Dockers, a baseball from your hometown team, and chocolate for the family. It's also customary to make a cash donation after the surrogate has given birth. These gifts are in addition to the clinic fees. Dr. Patel had been careful to explain all this to me beforehand. Gifts at the first meeting help to break the ice, but it should not be cash. I went back and forth for ages about what to bring. Nothing I could give would fully convey my appreciation. I mean, what do you give to the woman who may carry your child for you?

"And your husband?" I can tell by the look in her eyes that she's not afraid of him. I am relieved to see this.

"He is a good man," she tells me through the translator. My eyes dart back and forth between Vaina and Ayisha. It's going to take me some time to get used to communicating via a third person.

"He is a laborer. I am a house cleaner. Sometimes I work at the textile mill sewing beads on saris. And I am a mama. We live in a village about fifty kilometers away, so my husband will bring the children and stay in Anand so they can come and visit me." She looks sad for a moment, but then shakes it off and smiles, and looks me in the eye for the first time. I smile back.

"So you are going to live with the other surrogates in the clinic apartments?" I ask, encouraged that she is beginning to open up a little.

"Yes, I feel this is very important for me and for my family," she answers, sounding a little scripted but also like she means it. She looks like a woman who knows her own mind. It's clear that Dr. Patel has talked to Vaina, as she does to all the surrogates, to clarify her role and manage her expectations. I can be confident that Vaina knows exactly what she's signed on for, just as I do. Though we are both wandering through the unknown—strangers in a strange land—this knowledge is very comforting.

"I have done surrogacy once before," Vaina says and her smile fades for a moment. "It was not successful, so I want to do everything to be sure we are successful this time." Vaina hadn't gotten pregnant the time before. Dr. Patel explained that the genetic mother had been much older, and her eggs had not been viable, so the failure had nothing to do with Vaina. Still, Vaina seems to feel somehow responsible, so I smile reassuringly to let her know I have confidence in her, and she smiles back.

"Are you…" I hesitate. I know that in some rural areas, areas like the one that Vaina probably comes from, surrogates are considered to be on the same level with sex trade workers. This is another important reason for providing a surrogate house for the surrogates while they are in the program. In this way, the surrogates can remain anonymous, and return to their lives without any repercussions. I want to be sure that what we're doing isn't going to put her in any danger.

"Are you comfortable being a surrogate? Are you afraid of what might happen if people in your village found out?"

Vaina pauses and then shakes her head no. She smiles, and I believe her. Her smile is not enigmatic, but sweet and uncomplicated. She doesn't tell me anything more, but I can sense her inner calm, and I feel very relieved.

The translator indicates that it's time to wrap things up. I kiss Vaina lightly on the cheek and tell her once again how grateful I feel for what she is doing for us. I will see her again soon. Vaina smiles shyly, and looks uncomfortable, but tells me that she is happy to meet me and help me to have a happy family like she has. And then, just as suddenly as it began, our first meeting is abruptly over.

❋❀❀❋

I stumble into the lobby, a little dazed from so many intense and conflicting emotions coursing through my system along with the IVF hormones. I see that Abhi is leaning jauntily against the front desk, chatting up the receptionist with the movie star smile. As soon as he sees me, he rushes toward me, arms outstretched. "Now we take you to the new hotel," he says, sweeping me, as if he were a whisk broom and I were dust, out of the clinic doors and into the rickshaw. "I've already delivered your bags," he says.

The Hotel Laksh is one of the nicer hotels in Anand, although at first glance it doesn't look much different from the last one. It certainly doesn't look like an upgrade. The front desk could be from any American economy motor lodge, but the bright, colorful, flower-power wallpaper that shouts from an accent wall beside it lets me know that this hotel is a bit different—like a Howard Johnson's redesigned by hippies.

The lobby is crowded with couples from all over the world. The dining room looks like a Benetton ad, couples all engaged in friendly but intense conversations in small clusters here and there. The talk is lively, but I can tell by the faces that these people have been through rocky terrain on the road to this hotel, just as I have. I feel as if I've arrived at summer camp a week late, and everyone's already picked out their bunkmate. Without Alex by my side, I feel even more alone and adrift. I have some serious catching up to do in order to fit in. But first, I better find my cabin.

I check in at the front desk. The girl who helps me is very kind, with large, dark eyes and a shiny black plait down the center of her back. She reminds me in some ways of a younger Vaina. I can't get Vaina's face out of my mind. The concierge tells me that my bags are already in the room, hands me a key, and tells me to stop by the desk if I have any questions.

"Is there a working air-conditioner?" I ask. I've already learned what's really important and what isn't.

"Yes, definitely, in the rooms there is air-conditioning," she says. I could have kissed her. My room turns out to be a business suite, which means the bathroom and bedroom are in separate alcoves, joined by a little sitting area where an air-conditioner hums unreliably. Bold colors clash on the walls. Between the noise, the colors, and the medications I'm now taking, I should have a terrible headache, but instead I feel overwhelmed with delight in my new home. It's peaceful here, and there's *air-conditioning*!

I immediately collapse onto the bed, utterly exhausted. No sooner have I crashed, though, than I am startled by someone barging into my room. This time, it is not Abhi. Knocking before entering is still, sadly, a very American thing that I don't seem to find often in Anand.

"Hi, I'm Alyssa," says a spirited Jamaican woman who walks right in and extends her hand to me jovially.

"I'm Adrienne," I say, swinging my legs to the floor. "Nice to meet you." I suddenly understand how Vaina must have felt this afternoon. Alyssa is a lot to take in, a vibrant abundance of commitment and enthusiasm and exuberance, all pulled together in a very brightly colored sari.

"This your first time, sweetheart?" Alyssa asks bluntly, making herself at home on the foot of my bed and putting her hand on my leg conspiratorially. If I am the new camper, she is clearly the den mother.

"Yes," I say a little tentatively. "You?"

Alyssa shakes her head in that way that says this is definitely not her first experience. "No, second," she says, smiling wistfully. "The first time the IVF didn't work for me, but, well, what can you do? I'm not getting any younger, you know!"

Wait, what did she say? This was the second time today that I had met somebody whose first try had been unsuccessful. I wanted this to work for me the *first time*. Of course, my plan always included the possibility of going back for a second round of IVF, but Alex and I had decided after that, we would adopt. Alex was already checking out a few international adoption programs in Russia. We were keeping all our options open, but I still hoped against hope that my IVF would be successful on the first try, and that Vaina would soon be pregnant with my child. I was so eager to be a mom, I couldn't bear any more false starts.

"Don't worry, you are much younger than me," Alyssa says, obviously noticing that my mind has wandered off somewhere. "I've waited fourteen years to have a baby. But this time, it's going to be charmed. My surrogate is four months pregnant now, and I'm not leaving until that baby is born!"

"Are you and your surrogate..." I struggle to find the right words. I'm thinking of how distant and intermittently uncomfortable my first meeting with Vaina had just been, and how much I want to feel connected with her. "Are you friends?"

"Don't worry," Alyssa says, gently urging me to lie back on the bed and propping a pillow under my head. "Once you two get to know each other, you will be just fine. After all, you both want the same thing, yes?"

I nod my head, unable to shake off the new feelings of doubt. My eyes are misting, and I am as weary as I've been in weeks. It's been a long day.

"Get some rest now," says Alyssa, and I listen to her. She strikes me as a woman who knows what she is talking about. Her voice is so soothing and her attention so caring. I know she will be a good mother. "We'll talk later. Lord knows I'm not going anywhere. So we will have plenty of time! Here is my local mobile. Call me whenever you need a chat." And with that, Alyssa floats out of the room and shuts the door. At that very moment, the air-conditioner coughs, sputters, and completely shuts down.

This day has been more challenging and surprising than I ever would have expected, but now, in my new hotel room, I feel connected to something larger than myself. I'm now part of a community made up of people like Alyssa—genetic moms and dads from all over the world, all gathered here for the same reason, to make a future for their families. Abhi was right, Anand is beginning to feel a little bit like home.

As I shut my eyes and drift off to sleep, I hear the Muslim prayers, carried on the hot afternoon breeze like a sacred silk thread, reminding me and everyone who listens that we are all connected; that no matter where you wander, you are an integral part of something larger than you can fully comprehend; that no matter how much loss one endures, life carries on; and that, of course, God is everywhere.

※﹪※﹪※

Later that afternoon, I return to the clinic for my second round of fertility shots. I don't even see Dr. Patel; this time I go straight to the nurses with the needles. I'm quickly becoming a pro. Abhi drives me back to my hotel in time for dinner, and I decide to eat in the dining room with the other guests.

Alyssa is the center of the action, moving here and there to put a comforting arm around someone or to add a little humor into a particularly heavy conversation. She seems like such a natural mother: beaming, all-powerful, omnipresent. She turns from her conversation and opens her arms to welcome me as I walk into the dining room.

"Hello, Adrienne. I heard you just started your IVF today. How are you feeling, darling?" she asks, pulling out a chair for me.

"I'm fine, a little woozy," I say, realizing that I am a bit dizzy. It could be hunger, or the shots, which I will now receive twice a day for the next fourteen days, but I think that it's also the overwhelming effect of all these smiling, warm faces, all turned toward me. "I feel like so much has happened today!" I take a seat among the group and pick up the menu. I don't recognize a single word.

"The restaurant is vegetarian," says Gilde, a pretty blond

woman at the table, who is sitting next to her husband, Arthur. "I would recommend sticking with the lentils. It doesn't pay to get too adventurous on your first day, or it could be a long two weeks of morning shots. Take it from someone who knows," Gilde says, and gives me a sisterly wink.

Gilde and Arthur, I learn, are here from Germany. They and their surrogate gave birth to a healthy baby boy over a year ago. They have been in Anand since then, trying to arrange a visa to go home. The child was refused German citizenship and entry into the country, since surrogacy is not recognized in Germany. According to German law, the boy was not their son. Since then, the new parents had literally set up shop, hiring a lawyer to fight the German courts for recognition, with no choice but to wait in Anand for the red tape to unravel. They had become the expert authorities on exit visas in Surrogacy Camp. They told me that in order to get one for my baby, I would need to make an appointment at the local police station and present the following paperwork: a surrogacy agreement between the applicant surrogate mother and doctor treating the case, a letter from the hospital where the baby was born, an application for the infant's passport, a birth certificate for my baby issued by an Indian authority, both parents' passports and copies of our visas, airline tickets for the parents and the baby, three copies of the baby's photo with a white background, and a "no objection" letter from the surrogate mother. They also told me that for U.S. citizens, the paperwork takes anywhere from one to ten days to process. Listening to Gilde and Arthur's careful instructions and their incredible story somewhat unnerves me. I had not taken exit visa problems into account. What would Alex and I do if this happened to us?

Also at the table is a woman named Juliet, a Manhattanite who has undergone unsuccessful IVF nine times in the last fifteen years. Finally she came to Akanksha and used an Indian egg donor as her surrogate and egg donor, and thankfully, it worked the first time. Egg donation, when local women donate their eggs to infertile couples and single women, is yet another big business in India. Juliet has moved to India and is spending the entire pregnancy here in Anand with her surrogate. I wonder what strange effect rural India is having on all of these metropolitan people. I had heard before I came that many women go home between the IVF procedure and the birth of their child, and yet all of these people seem to have relocated to Anand, the milk capital of India. Will this happen to me too?

At the end of the table is a couple from Dubai. The husband seems very laid-back and sweet, and his wife is adorable. Alyssa tells me that IVF had failed three times for them, so this time they are doing surrogacy simultaneously in three different clinics, just to be on the safe side.

"Is that legal?" I ask Alyssa, a little shocked. Alyssa shrugs her shoulders.

"The regulations of surrogacy are not keeping up with the demand for surrogates. People are very poor here, and competition between clinics is high. Even if the doctors know that their patients are working with another clinic simultaneously, they will look the other way. They don't want to say no to the money."

Here in India, rules are made to be bent, and laws are made to be broken. I can't help but worry about this couple—how will they maintain relationships with three surrogates? And how will they raise three new babies? But in a sense, we are all rule benders here in Surrogacy Camp. We have all been through terrible loss and heartache, and we have all made difficult choices in order to be here. We are all defying the odds and trying to have a family, no matter what anybody else has to say about it. And India has made that possible too.

1. http://news.bbc.co.uk/2/hi/6086334.stm, October 26, 2006.
2. http://topics.nytimes.com/top/opinion/editorialsandoped/oped/columnists/nicholasdkristof/index.html?scp=1&sq=kristoff%20india&st=cse.
3. http://www.nytimes.com/2011/05/26/opinion/26kristof.html?_r=1&ref=nicholasdkristof
4. http://www.csrindia.org/index.php/girls-education.

chapter 5

Day 2 of my two-week IVF treatment cycle, and I am *starving*. This is not your typical, oh, I'm so hungry, I could really go for a greasy cheeseburger. This is serious. I could eat the curtains.

Before I left San Francisco, friends and acquaintances horrified me with grim tales about the agonies of IVF, and to be honest, I have been dreading the experience. The nausea, the mood swings, the sore muscles, the painful shots: they made it sound just a few steps shy of the seventh circle of hell. One of my friends told me she'd been so rattled by the hormones that she'd punched her husband in the face. I didn't mention this anecdote to Alex.

Fortunately, I'm not feeling combative, and even if I were, my husband is eight thousand miles away. The shots really do hurt, as everyone had told me they would, and I feel crummy. Who knows if it's the heat or the exotic food, or the complete and utter lack of any red wine within a hundred-mile radius, or the IVF. It's my new normal, a generalized Indian malaise. Except that today, I am ravenous in a town where the superstar of most menus is lentils. It's a new low.

I start to cry. I'm safe in my bed, the morning prayers are wafting on the breeze, and everything is going exactly as planned. I have nothing to complain about and the fact that even when everything is going right I still feel sad, just makes me cry harder. I have to be showered, dressed, and out on the street hailing a rickshaw to the clinic in half an hour to get my next shot. Dr. Patel does not like to be kept waiting, but I'm so hungry and sore, I can hardly think. I reach for the phone.

"Hi, Adrienne, how are you doing today, my love?" my husband asks. His voice is even and calm and comforting, which means he must know that I'm upset even though I haven't said anything yet.

"Alex, I'm hungry," I whine, realizing as I say it that I sound like an irritating five-year-old.

"So order some food," says Alex, still soothing, even though I've probably caught him in the midst of fourteen workplace catastrophes, all of which he is handling without shedding a single tear.

"I'm sorry, I'm just feeling emotional, and I don't know why. "

"Adrienne. You're in India, alone, going through IVF."

"Oh yeah," I say, beginning to laugh at myself, thinking about how lucky I am to have such a sweet and patient husband, and then I start to cry again. If it keeps up like this, it's going to be a very soggy two weeks.

"Listen," says Alex, taking matters into his own hands, "I'm going to call my mom, and she's going to come to Anand to keep you company. I can't get over there myself for a week, but my mom will be thrilled and be with you within forty-eight hours. I'll take care of everything. You just relax, and order yourself some eggs."

"Don't say eggs. I am focusing too much on my own eggs." I laugh. "And don't call your mother. I'm fine." I'm so accustomed to being rational, focused, and able to handle difficult situations solo. In fact, I prefer it. I'm now a bit embarrassed about my outburst. It isn't at all like me to be so . . . well . . . *emotional.*

"Adrienne, we all know you are a solid citizen, but right now it sounds like you are springing a few leaks, and no wonder. My mom's been chomping at the bit to be a part of this process and spend some time with you anyway. I'll let you know what she says. Call me when you leave the clinic. Now order some breakfast already!" I can hear the smile in his voice, and I'm overpowered by a deep longing for him.

After we hang up, I feel worlds better. Talking to Alex always has that effect on me. As embarrassed as I am at the idea of Alex's mom potentially flying across the world to help me—shouldn't I be able to figure out my breakfast on my own?—I am also a little excited at the thought of seeing Jenny. We have both been waiting for the right opportunity to spend some time together, and this is certainly unconventional, but the idea of her holding my hand when I go for my next round of shots fills me with relief.

I pick up the phone and try to order eggs, which is easier said than done. Anand is strictly vegetarian, and eggs are *illegal* in this small town. Ordering eggs in Anand is like ordering marijuana in New York City: if you call the right number, you can have them delivered directly to your doorstep, but you have to eat them in your room, in private where no one will see you, and you should try to keep the smell out of your clothes. For a country that is so permissive about surrogacy laws, they certainly are uptight about their eggs. And, as with anything on the black market, there's no telling what will actually arrive when you order them. Eggs are such a foreign concept to most cooks in Anand, there's no telling what is *really* lurking underneath the cream sauce. It's a culinary crapshoot, but I am a gambler at heart. And I'm ravenous. So, this morning, as I will every morning that follows, I roll the dice and I order two of them, with Indian coffee and a *dosa*, which is like a large Indian crepe made with rice flour. I jump in the shower with my fingers crossed and shortly thereafter, my breakfast arrives. Not an egg in sight. Just a very suspicious-looking curry sauce, with a couple of lumps in the middle that are definitely *not* eggs. I could cry; another crushing defeat in my daily game of breakfast roulette. But I'm too hungry and too late for the clinic to mourn for long. I wolf down the dosa and a few sips of coffee and sprint out to find a rickshaw to the clinic. Abhi is picking up another genetic mother at the airport today, so I'm forced to fend for myself.

The morning streets are bustling with the completely unchoreographed chaos of Anand at rush hour. Luck is with me, and I'm able to hail a rickshaw right away. My stomach is in knots. I focus on the traffic, not on the dosa doing flips in my stomach, and will the crowds to part, the way they do whenever I travel with Abhi. I am quite delighted to discover that it works.

I arrive at the clinic in ten short minutes—blissfully on time—and take a seat in the hallway outside the medical procedure room to wait for my morning shots. Sitting in the hall with me are a number of couples I recognize from the hotel. Everybody is talking about eggs, but not the kind I *didn't* just have for breakfast. This conversation is all about follicles, progesterone, and how many eggs each woman has managed to produce. I eavesdrop for a moment and discover that Carlotta, who is my age, has four eggs, which is pretty good. Lynette has six, which is outstanding, and I think I detect a note of jealousy in the crowd as she announces her stellar sum. Poor Jeanette, who is older, has only two eggs, which is apparently very bad, but everybody clucks and puts their collective arm around her and reassures her that all it takes is one, before imperceptibly shrinking away from her, as if her bad luck is contagious.

We, all of us huddled in this shabby but friendly corridor in this remote oasis of hope on the Pakistani border, have come for the same reason. We are all out on a limb but determined to hold on until we are able to have a child of our own. Because we are all swinging from a thin branch over an unthinkable abyss, there is an air of urgency, a singularity of focus; if we take our eyes off the branch for one moment, we'll fall.

The desperation in this hallway is palpable, and even though I know that Alex and I have other options available to us, I too have moved away from Jeanette. After so many disappointments, I know I shouldn't want this so badly. But I just can't help it.

"Hi, I'm Caroline," says a pleasant, albeit tense-looking woman beside me. She must not like needles either.

"I'm Adrienne," I say and hold out my hand, which I realize too late is slightly damp. Caroline takes my hand; her palm is damp too. We are sisters joined by a common anxiety.

"I'm Cyril," says her husband, with a sly grin that I like instantly. "And just in case you were wondering, we have three eggs."

At this point I laugh much too loud, and all eyes immediately turn toward me. I realize that I haven't had a genuine, good laugh since I left San Francisco, and this morning in particular has been crying out, literally, for a little comic relief. I may be inappropriate for a waiting room, but laughing is better than counting eggs.

"Nice to meet you," I whisper, trying to shake off the unwanted attention I've drawn to myself with my outburst. (I'm famous for moments like this.)

"Have you just started?" says Caroline.

"Yesterday," I say. "I guess you can tell I'm the new kid in town."

"We all were not too long ago," Caroline says sweetly. "How are you feeling?"

"Hungry," I say, realizing that my stomach is growling again.

"Cracker?" Caroline says, digging in her purse and coming up with a packet of saltines. "I've learned not to leave home without them."

"You're a lifesaver," I say, and greedily stuff several in my mouth. Grief—unexpected and powerful—hits me like a sledgehammer. This moment—feeling slightly nauseous, tired, mouth full of saltines—reminds me of how I felt when I was pregnant. My eyes well with tears. Not two minutes ago, I brought attention to myself for laughing, and now I will have to run out of the clinic before everyone sees me crying.

"Atrief? Atrief Aref?" I realize that this indecipherable jumble of vowels consonants is my name, which sounds wildly different every time somebody attempts to say it in this town . . . kind of like with the eggs. So I have to pay attention.

"Yes?" I say, a little apprehensively, standing up.

"The doctor will see you now," says the nurse at the far end of the hallway. I blink back the tears, smile at my new friends, screw up some courage, and head down that long corridor toward whatever is waiting for me at the other end. Whatever it is, I know it will include needles. When I reach the nurse, she smiles, and without any warning at all, plunges one needle into my right arm and another into my left. It's over before I even have time to react. I'm starting to appreciate the wisdom of the clinic's surprise attack methods—they move in quickly and disappear without leaving a trace.

Next, I'm politely ushered into a larger room, this one filled with surrogates and genetic moms, all sitting on metal examining tables equipped with stirrups, and attended to by the lightning-quick nurses, who are mostly dressed in richly colored saris, though some are in scrubs, and move about the room as gracefully and quietly as dancers, delivering care with a comfortable and almost sacred efficiency.

"Good morning, Adrienne, how are you feeling?" asks Dr. Patel, suddenly appearing at my side with her sunrise of a smile and the sonogram wand poised in her hand.

"I'm fine, a little hungry and weepy," I say, letting her lay me back to get ready for my sonogram.

"Yes, well that is very normal," she says pleasantly. "Everybody goes through something with the IVF, some more, some less, but everybody feels a little vulnerable because of the hormone injections. You will be all right?" she asks, and waits, and I know there is only one answer I can possibly give her, because of course, she's right. I'm fine.

"I'll be all right," I say, and somehow, just in saying it aloud, I convince myself it's true.

"Good," says Dr. Patel, moving on and ever efficient. Dr. Patel has a roomful of women requiring her attention most of the hours of every day. Moving on is her middle name.

"Let's see what we've got now," she says, and begins running the cold sensor a little roughly over my stomach. Her touch is not exactly gentle, but I forgive her. I know that her equipment, while perfectly functional, is not state-of-the-art whisper-touch technology. I can handle a bit of prodding. I tense as the images on the screen come into view. In my experience, sonograms are forever connected to disappointment, grief, and indescribable despair. They always remind me of how much I've lost, always make me think of Colette.

I hold my breath, waiting for her to find something wrong. Her face furrows with concentration and discontent. She sees it right away. It is, after all, the reason I am here.

"You have very large fibroid tumors," she says, and shuts off the machine. I sit up so that we can talk face-to-face.

"Yes, is that going to be a problem?" I ask, feeling suddenly shaky and fragile. I want this to work so badly.

"No, no problem with egg production, but the IVF treatment could cause the tumors to grow larger. We'll keep our eye on it," she says, stroking my arm reassuringly. "You have four, maybe five follicles developing. That is very good."

Four, maybe five. Not too many, not too few, but just right. I am giddy with relief and my knees go a little weak when I stand up. The nurse steadies me, and I go out to greet another hormone-saturated day, which, like most days for me in Anand, dawned without my having the slightest idea of where I would go or what I would do, aside from my daily visit to the clinic. I know one thing, though. Whatever this day brings me, it's going to have to include some junk food.

I say goodbye to Caroline and Cyril, tell them I will see them back at the hotel later, and make my way out into the searing heat. The only thing I want to do at this moment is to go back to the hotel, rest and relax, eat something—*anything*—and call Alex. Four or five eggs! I hail a rickshaw and begin a very vivid and absorbing daydream about tearing into the Toblerone bar back in my room, when my cell rings. It's Alex.

"Hey, babe," he says, "how'd everything go?" It takes me a minute to answer because I am still utterly captivated by thoughts of chocolate, my reward for producing all these follicles. Also, I'm in a rickshaw in downtown Anand at noon, and in case I haven't said it before, it's really, *really* hot.

"Adrienne?" Alex says, sounding worried.

"Sorry, sorry, Alex, I'm fine. I'm on my way back to the hotel. Everything went great. Dr. Patel says my tumors are big."

"Your what?" he says, unable to hear me over the wail of a police siren that passes by at just that moment.

"My fibroid tumors are really big!" I yell into the phone, trying my best to be heard over the hubbub. And just then, the siren goes quiet and all traffic comes to a halt. Crickets. My voice carries out into the suddenly silent street, letting everyone within a three-mile radius know about the size of my uterine fibroids. I would die of embarrassment, but nobody even seems to notice.

"Well, is that going to be a problem?" Alex asks, and I can hear the slight tremor of terror in his voice. He doesn't want to relive last year either. He wants this to work as much as I do.

"She doesn't seem too worried. We just have to keep our eye on it."

Alex audibly exhales. "That is good news. Hey, I talked to my mom, she was able to get a flight out!"

"Wow! That's fast!" I say, and smile. Jenny is a kind and gentle woman, but her sweet demeanor belies a will of true iron. Jenny was born and spent her earliest years in war-torn Glasgow, during the Nazi bombings. She was raised on war rations, and family lore holds that she once finished an entire month's ration of chocolate while riding on the back of her mother's bicycle as they returned from the grocery store. Even after all her years in California, she still retains that gorgeous Scottish accent; listening to her is a form of meditation.

The rest of the day is spent in a Toblerone-induced sugar coma, from which I emerge just as the sun begins to set. I discover that the air-conditioner in my room has heaved and belched its last misty puff of tepid air. Even though I never opened a window, the mosquitoes have somehow, mysteriously, found a way in, and it's gotten so bad that I now sleep under a mosquito net in my hotel bed. The time has come to call in reinforcements.

So, I do what I have learned to do whenever I run into a bump on the road in India. I call Abhi, who knows everything about everything, and everybody who can do something about it.

Abhi comes to my room later that evening, surveys my room, floor strewn with chocolate wrappers, and sees the mosquito net. He shakes his head and begins to laugh.

"Chu no need that net for mosquitoes," he says, explaining the facts of life to me slowly, as if I am a child. "It is low season. These mosquitoes will fly in other parts."

"Tell that to the fourteen mosquitoes that bit me last night," I say, sounding a little more annoyed than I mean to. I know he's just trying to be positive and calm me down, but these are not American mosquitoes; the bites are already turning into welts. I must be quite a sight: a crazy American lady, scratching at angry bumps all over her arms and legs, with chocolate in the corner of her mouth, constantly on the verge of tears, intermittently banging on the air-conditioner as if she could force the great beast back to life with tiny angry fists. I'm a hot mess.

"I know the owner. I will talk to him, " says Abhi. "They will get this working for you, no charge," he says magnanimously. "In the meantime, I will take you to a nice place my friend owns for dinner. He has very good dinner there."

"Thank you, Abhi," I say, feeling very relieved and grateful for Abhi's all-embracing, all-knowing resourcefulness, even if he is dead wrong about those mosquitoes.

"Stay with me and the gods will be with you," Abhi says with a wink, and dials a number and starts barking at someone on the other end. While Abhi lays down the law, I slather my ankles with calamine lotion.

Before I leave for dinner, I stop off at the desk and leave the address of the restaurant for Jenny with the girl with the beautiful braid, who I now know is called Fatima.

"My mother-in-law is meeting me here. Can you give her this

note, please, so she'll know where to meet me?" I ask Fatima slowly, and a little too loudly. Fatima smiles and nods her head. "Yes," she says, and then, "God be with you."

Abhi drives me the short distance to the restaurant and talks to his friend, and a plate is brought out for me. Settled at last, I read my book and wait for Jenny. And I wait. And I wait some more. I'm just beginning to worry when my cell phone rings.

"Adrienne, where are you? My mom is at the hotel and thinks you've panicked and skipped town," Alex says with a tinge of annoyance in his voice.

"I'm sorry, the air-conditioner broke in my room, so I'm at a restaurant until they fix it. I left a note for Jenny at the front desk. Tell her to sit tight; I'm on my way."

A few minutes later I am back at the hotel, and there is Jenny, looking exhausted and limp from the heat, but it is such a joy to see her face; she has never looked so beautiful.

"Adrienne! Oh, thank goodness. I'm so happy to see you! I thought you'd cut and run, and who could blame you in this heat? Poor thing, absolutely dreadful in this country this time of year. Oh, how lovely, it's just us girls at last. Thank you so much for letting me come and share this special time with you, and how wonderful to be back in India again. I haven't been here since I was pregnant with Alex. But enough for the stroll down memory lane, when can we eat? I'm starving!"

And although I have only just left a restaurant and a full meal, the idea of food sounds fantastic. Once we have both gone to our rooms to freshen up a bit, we head out to the singular rooftop restaurant in town.

"I'll have the *dal makhani*," I say, predictably. Since arriving in Anand, I've eaten this dish of lentils and rice at virtually every meal. It's safe, mercifully predictable, and I'm low on Pepto.

Jenny, ever adventurous, rattles off a string of words that I don't understand, and when our food arrives, she generously offers me little bites of everything. Her food, unlike mine, is alternately spicy, sour, sweet, or tart.

"So, I've been thinking," Jenny says with a mischievous look in her eye that I know very well, "we ought to do a little traveling while I'm here, Adrienne." She takes a tentative taste of something called *parwal korma,* a dish involving what looks to be disintegrating pumpkin, swimming in a viscous saffron-colored sauce. For all my international travel, I'm not a particularly adventurous eater, and this rather squishy and jiggly dish does not look the least bit inviting, but Jenny takes another little bite, sighs with appreciation, and then moves on to the next mystery dish. All the while, she expands upon her plan for the next week of my life. She is a strategist of the first order.

"We need to take your mind off things. It's the best thing. If I'm not mistaken, Barola is very close. There's a lovely park there, perfect for a day trip. And perhaps we could get your friend Mr. Abhi to take us up to Udaipur in Rajasthan for a couple of days. It's absolutely breathtaking up there. Lovely castles and nature walks; it's known as the City of Lakes."

"Oh, I wish I could, Jenny, but I have to be at the clinic every morning for my shots," I say, genuinely dismayed. I'd love to be a tourist, and I'd love to avoid bursting into tears in the waiting room as I did this morning in front of the other patients, but this is simply too important for me to give up now.

"Oh we can find a way around that," says Jenny, spearing a piece of suspicious-looking fried cheese and popping it into her mouth. "I'm a biologist, after all; I know how to work a syringe. We'll just take the injections with us. I'm sure we can round up a cooler or something, and then we'll be free to wander wherever the wind takes us. We'll just stay perpetually in transit.

Time will fly, and Alex will be here before you know it. My, isn't the cashew curry delicious!"

How could you not love this woman? With her by my side, I immediately feel braver, stronger, more like the woman I was when I left San Francisco. After our meal, we return to the hotel to rest and plan our adventure. It turns out that it's just as Jenny had predicted—the clinic is able to give me my medications, syringes, and any other supplies we may need with little fanfare or complication. Finding a cooler turns out to be a bit more difficult, but Abhi proves yet again to be an absolute gem. Within one day, we are quite literally on our way.

Jenny and I take a day trip to Barola, and watch Indian families playing ball in the park. It proves to be a strikingly different scene from what I am used to in the States. There are no picnic baskets, no McDonald's bags or beer cans, no smoking barbecue grills, no ice cream carts, no boom boxes.

"It's very lovely," I say to Jenny. I'm having a rare moment when I can step outside my body—and all my raging hormones and expanding fibroid tumors, not to mention my free-floating anxiety—and am able, for an instant anyway, to fully appreciate the moment. "It's beautiful. Just families, enjoying the day, enjoying each other, without any distractions. It's so simple, isn't it?"

"Yes, it is. Everything worthwhile is, in the end, very simple. When you don't have a lot of stuff getting in the way, it makes it easier to fully enjoy what's really important. Less is more in India, no question about that."

I feel flooded with a feeling of utter calm and appreciation. "I'm glad we're spending this time together, Jenny. It means so much to have you here, to share this experience with me. Thank you so much for coming," I say, suddenly very grateful for her quiet, comforting presence.

"It's a total pleasure," Jenny says, and takes my hand. "I'm really glad to be here with you. And I'm so glad to be able to be here, since your mom can't be. I know she would have wanted to share this special experience with you too." Jenny, always warm and kind, but rarely visibly emotional, tears up and pulls me into a tight hug. I have been missing my mother for weeks now, and it is so comforting to be with another mother, some, one who knew and loved mine. It's also an incredible relief to have somebody else tearing up instead of just me. Weepy loves company.

❧ ❧❧❧ ❧

The next day, Jenny gets me up early, and we are on the move. We pack a couple of days' worth of shots in our cooler and set out with Abhi for Rajasthan, which is east, located in the foothills of the Aravalli Range. Abhi has found us a "good deal" with one of his "friends" at what turns out to be a stun, ning three,star hotel. After all my battles with recalcitrant air, conditioners and voracious mosquitoes, I'm in the mood to be pampered. I can almost feel the massage I am going to have as soon as we check in.

Upon arrival, we get settled and then go for a long walk to stretch our legs. It was a long, dusty ride from Anand. We dis, cover a garden of local spices and succulents, and Jenny stops and marvels at every plant and unusual flower and reads the labels. The spicy air smells delicious. Next we visit the Lake Palace, which was built by King Maharana Udai Singh (1522–72). Legend holds that Singh encountered a hermit in the forest, who told him that if he built a city in that very spot, it would always be safe. The king moved his royal residence to this place, and the palace stands to this day, unharmed and intact. With the beautiful lake stretching to the very tiptoes of the foothills, and the peaks of the Aravalli mountains towering beyond, and the gentle flow of Jenny's stories enveloping me like a blanket of love and protection, I feel calm and at peace. I am safe here.

The full course of my fertility drug treatment is eleven days, so in between walkabouts with Jenny, I continue to schedule regular checkups at the clinic with Dr. Patel. At last count, I had five follicles. I'm told that this is all that I will probably produce, but that's fine because Dr. Patel tells me that five is plenty. As all the genetic mothers in Surrgacy Camp remind me, and each other, and I suspect themselves every day, it only takes one egg. The Lupron and Zoladex are also causing my fibroid tumors to grow very quickly. I have four tumors now, each about the size of an orange, which is scary to think about. They're becoming increasingly uncomfortable for me. I feel hot and then cold; bloated beyond belief and yet hungry all the time. I'm literally counting the minutes until Alex arrives and we can extract and fertilize the eggs and be done with this leg of the journey.

Finally, day 8 of IVF dawns, and I feel like a little kid on her birthday. Alex is arriving later this evening, so I just do whatever I can to make the time pass quickly. But it doesn't. The minutes pass like hours. I finish my workout, go for a walk, try to do a little shopping, but my heart isn't in it. Then I go back to my room and try to read but mostly wait, wait, and wait. Occasionally I doze off and then wake up and wait some more. Finally, night falls, and my husband walks through the door with a great big smile, a great big kiss, and a great big bottle of duty-free scotch for Abhi. I think that I am going to burst with excitement. My adorable, unshakable, slightly right of center, but entirely lovable husband has finally arrived. I throw my arms around him and of course, start to cry, and Alex starts to laugh, but I think I see a tear or two forming in the corners of his eyes. Jenny runs into our room at that moment and throws her arms around both of us, and we are all a happy, soggy mess. Eventually, Alex pulls himself free, pours himself a stiff drink—smart man, he stocked up at duty-free—and says, "So, ladies, where are we having dinner?"

It's Jenny's last night in India, and Alex's first, so I want to take them out for an extra-special dinner. Anand is not exactly a culinary mecca, unless you really, *really* like Indian ice cream (which is rich and creamy, but tastes slightly sour to me—definitely not like the Ben and Jerry's I'm used to!). We choose an intriguing safari-inspired restaurant called the Jungle, which some of the other moms at the clinic have told me is an "experience." Honestly, with these two by my side, the hotel's room service "eggs" would be special, but the Jungle turns out to be not just unique but, like its theme, pretty wild, in that there is chicken on the menu. Actual nonvegetarian chicken. I think that this must be a Class B felony in these parts, and like a junkie ready for her fix, I can't wait to gorge myself on such a forbidden delight.

By the time the chicken arrives, which looks suspiciously like eggplant, if you ask me, the jet lag hits Alex, and he practically falls asleep in his *palak paneer*. We finish up our meal as quickly as we can and catch a rickshaw back to the hotel. Alex falls into the bed like a felled redwood.

"I love you, Alex, and I'm so happy you're here," I tell him, and kiss his cheek as he begins to snore softly beside me. For the first time since arriving in India, I feel like I'm home.

chapter 6

Alex sleeps for fifteen hours straight, only pulling himself out of bed to say good-bye to Jenny. As Jenny throws the last few things into her bag, Abhi arrives to take Alex and me to the clinic. Arrivals and departures are always overlapping in this village, where everyone is coming and going; it is often hard to get one's bearings. Poor Alex looks like a rickshaw hit him. He doesn't deal with time changes well, and I know all he wants to do is go back to bed, but he is in India now and must get used to being carried along by the inescapable, undeniable current of Indian life. And, like me, he must bend himself to the demands of Dr. Patel's schedule, whether he likes it or not.

"Thank you, Abhi, for taking such good care of us," Jenny says, and gives him a big hug before doing a final check for her ticket and her passport. Jenny always feels like she's forgotten something when she's leaving someplace, generally because she always has. I make a mental note to check her room before turning in her room key. I know that I will find some overlooked essential. I take it as her way of saying *I'll be back soon.*

"God go with you," says Abhi, laughing as usual. "And next time, you bring your husband."

"He could never keep up with me," says Jenny and turns to Alex and me, putting a hand on each of our shoulders. "Now, you two take good care of each other. And don't worry. Everything is going to work out wonderfully, I just know it. Keep me posted on all, and enjoy India! Don't spend all your time moping in that hotel, and, Adrienne, stay out of the horrible gym, for goodness' sakes, go for a walk instead. This is a unique chapter in your lives, so make the most of it! You're going to have to tell this story until you're blue in the face for years to come, and my, wasn't that cashew curry delicious? I must learn how to make it at home. See if you can get the recipe from that chef. I think he liked you. " And with that, Jenny climbs into her car, waves once, and disappears almost instantly into the riptide of the Anand streets.

"Abhi, this is my husband, Alex." I know Abhi has been wondering where my husband has been these last two weeks. "He just arrived last night." Abhi smiles, and not just his usual smile, but a smile that lets me know that he's genuinely pleased that at long last, Alex has finally come. Abhi doesn't think that women should be moving about willy-nilly, unaccompanied by a man. I try to forgive him. Abhi is, after all, a Hindu man with many daughters.

"Very nice to meet chu, boss, very glad chu could come to be with Atreene," says Abhi, and smiles at me and raises his eyebrows, waiting for me to agree, which of course, I do. Abhi laughs and puts his arm around Alex and gives him a vigorous clap on the shoulder. Alex, still a bit dazed from lack of sleep, looks vaguely uncomfortable for a moment, but he recovers quickly, takes Abhi's hand, and shakes it vigorously.

"Nice to meet you, Abhi," says Alex. "I want to thank you for taking such good care of Adrienne." This is exactly the right thing to say. Abhi throws his arms around Alex again and laughs and laughs. I can tell that Abhi instantly loves Alex with an affection that he has never quite managed to muster for me. It must be a guy thing.

"Should we go? I don't want be late for Dr. Patel," I say, growing weary of the male bonding, especially since it appears Abhi has now totally won over Alex. The two of them are starting to look as chummy as two fraternity brothers, which I find suddenly very annoying. Maybe it's because they are delaying lunch. I swear, I am going to be the only Westerner who gains weight in India.

Invoking the wrath of Dr. Patel seems to break the spell, and Abhi springs into action, proudly holding the door of the rickshaw open for Alex to climb in for the very first time. Then he helps me up alongside Alex, and closes the door with more care and style than I've ever seen him manage before. He climbs behind the wheel and plunges into the flow of traffic, only to come within kissing distance of the truck in front of us. The bed of the truck is loaded down with several thousand pounds of bananas that look ready to topple at any moment, but Alex doesn't flinch. The man may be exhausted, but he remains fearless.

As we come into view of the clinic, I watch for Alex's reaction. I see him take in the inevitable family of beggars stretched out on a blanket in front of the main entrance, the insouciant cows, the cheerful but tired and peeling exterior. I relive my first moments there through my husband. I can see each detail register in his eyes, but unlike me, it never shows on his face.

"Well, they could use a paint job," Alex finally says once we are safely inside, with a mischievous grin. We both burst out laughing, causing the new group of couples waiting in the hallway to stare at us, which makes us giggle even more. In that instant I swear I have never loved him more; together, Alex and I will go through whatever comes.

I cling to moments of certainty like this. I wish I could grab this feeling and put it in my pocket, so that I could pull it out whenever the weather ahead looks ominous. Surrogacy, like pregnancy or adoption, is a process fraught with uncertainty. All the territory is uncharted, every experience brand-new, and there are few signs to tell you whether you are headed in the right direction or straight off a cliff. I keep reminding my-self, this is the most important journey I will ever take, and at the end of it, we will be parents. Or at least I hope we will.

The nurse calls Alex's name, and of course, she pronounces it correctly the very first time. Is Alex *really* that much easier than Adrienne? It is time for him to give us his "contribution." She leads him to a sinister-looking unmarked door and hands him a cup, a page of instructions, and something called a "moff rag" to wash up with. I don't even want to know why they call it that. I sit in the hallway to wait for my regular morning shots. I hope that Alex will be able to, ahem, *rise* to the occasion. He looked a little shaky on entry. A few minutes later, he sits down beside me, looking like he wants to take a shower.

"Everything come out okay?" It is just impossible not to make terrible puns at every turn during this process. I just can't seem to help myself. I'm still in seventh grade sometimes, what can I say? Alex blushes, and then Hitesh Patel, Dr. Patel's husband, who also works with patients here, chimes in, "Alex, you made a record! Long John Silver. In and out in two min-utes." Alex slumps in his seat, blushing profusely, fearless no more. He is ready to get out of here and by ready I mean like yesterday. The moff rag obviously really got to him.

"The aesthetics are really awful in there," he hisses. "I mean, couldn't they give you a magazine or *something* so you don't have to just stand there watching the paint chip?"

"I'm sorry, my love," I say, with genuine sympathy. "Think of it as taking one for the team."

"Next time they want a sample from me, we're doing it at the hotel. At least it has better lighting. And soap."

Finally, after what I'm sure must feel like an eternity for poor Alex, the nurse calls my name and I get my shots. We are then led into Dr. Patel's office for Alex to meet her. I've been looking forward to this moment with great anticipation since I arrived in India. Dr. Patel appears, as usual, in a swirl of good energy, rich color, and whispering sandals. She goes right up to Alex, gives him a big smile, and heartily shakes his hand.

"So nice to meet you in person, Alex, did you have a pleasant trip?"

"Yes, thank you, nice to meet you too," says Alex, who I can see realizes, just as I did, that he is shaking hands with a force of nature.

"I'll bet Adrienne was very happy to see you! She's been talking about nothing else for days," says Dr. Patel, winking and laying me back on the table for my sonogram.

"Well, I'm happy to be here, finally. It was very hard being so far away while Adrienne was going through all of this for us."

"Yes, very good that you are here now, and soon, you will be able to go home together and wait for your baby, God willing. So, Adrienne, let's see what we've got today. Lie back, please, and take a deep breath now."

Again the rough and cold sensor on my stomach as the blurry images flicker into view. What will we find today? I can tell Alex is poised for the worst, just as I am. I wonder if there will ever be a time when we can go through a sonogram without this remembered feeling of dread. I can see the tumors on the screen, and they terrify me with their size. I remember seeing those very same tumors during my first pregnancy, growing bigger every day, eventually producing heartbreak. I start to tear up. Perhaps noticing my distress, or perhaps just because she's seen enough, Dr. Patel switches off the machine.

"You can sit up now," she says, washing her hands behind

me. "You have five follicles. This is good for someone of your age." At thirty-six, I suddenly feel ancient.

"And the tumors?" says Alex. Dr. Patel furrows her brow and takes a breath. He's not a litigator for nothing. The man knows how to ask the tough questions. "Adrienne mentioned you were concerned about the uterine tumors. Have they gotten larger?"

"Yes," says Dr. Patel without missing a beat. "As I explained to Adrienne, tumors can grow as a result of this hormone treatment. There are four of them now, each about the size of an orange. But there is no immediate danger. You can follow up with your doctor when you get back home, Adrienne. After today's shots, we will skip a day of hormones, and then you will have a final shot at midnight to release the eggs. The following morning, we will do the egg retrieval."

I'm very relieved to hear that this part of the process is almost over, but I'm a little apprehensive about this midnight shot idea. I've heard about those shots. They call it the beesting shot, because it feels like you are being stung. Not by one bee, like when you get your ears pierced or have blood taken. Think an entire *hive* of bees. *This* is the shot that made my friend punch her husband in the eye. Again, I decide not to share this information with Alex. Between the masturbatory shame and news of my orange-size tumors, he is grappling with enough.

"When will the implantation happen?" asks Alex, still in lawyer mode.

"The day after the retrieval," says Dr. Patel. "You can, of course, attend if you like, but honestly it's a quick procedure and there's no reason for you to be present. You may find it better to spend that time traveling and seeing something of India before you return home. I will let you know in a few weeks if the IVF has been successful."

"How many embryos will you implant?" asks Alex, and this

stops me in my tracks for a second because I realize I haven't thought about this before. Visions of Kate Gosselin and Nadya Suleman, the infamous octomom, flood my brain. Given that nearly a third of traditional pregnancies end in miscarriage, it is typical for more than one fertilized egg to be implanted for an IVF pregnancy. But it is impossible to know how many fertilized embryos, if any, will survive and become healthy babies. What is the right number? Two, three, four? What happens if they *all* are viable? Alex and I have only thought about having one child; are we prepared for twins or triplets or—gulp—even more? Are there regulations here about how many eggs a doctor can implant? And what about Vaina? How many babies should she or would she be willing to carry to term? *Why don't I know this?* I look at Dr. Patel, who appears completely serene in the face of Alex's questions. She's obviously answered this question before.

"If we have many viable eggs, we will implant four," she says. "We will then wait to see what happens, and make our decision from there."

"What decision?" I ask, tentatively.

"The decision about whether or not to reduce," she explains. "The cold, hard facts are that the risks of complications for the surrogate and for the baby increase dramatically from a single child to twins, and multiply as you move on to triplets and beyond." Triplets and beyond? Alex looks at me, smiles reassuringly, and squeezes my hand. "We will make a decision that is in the best interests of the baby and the surrogate when the time comes."

So that was it. Egg retrieval, fertilization, and then back home to wait for whatever would happen. Alex and I leave the clinic feeling a little drained. There is always so much information to absorb and so many physical and ethical issues to deal with.

It can become positively exhausting. We had planned to spend our afternoon walking around Anand so I could show Alex all the sites, but this takes all of half an hour. We head back to the room to rest in the air-conditioning, think about everything Dr. Patel has told us, and catch up on some badly missed quality time. We don't talk much. We don't really have to. We know it all, without saying a word.

That night, we stroll through the silent streets of Anand after dark. We stop for one of the worst pizzas I have ever eaten in my life—why make a pizza without real cheese? And worse still, why did I try to eat it?—and then we visit the Ice Palace for two scoops of Anand's finest. I see the delight on the children's faces around me as they lick their cones, making me wish that my taste in ice cream wasn't quite so American. The Indian version looks like pure heaven in the mouths of the kids. When Alex and I get back to our hotel, the desk clerk stops to give us Jenny's book, which they found in the drawer beside her bed. Alex and I share a laugh over this vintage Jenny moment, before dropping into bed. We both sleep like the dead.

Day 11 of IVF begins early with an unexpected knock on the door. As I jump up to answer it, I realize that this day that is starting so early will end very late, with the midnight beesting shot of MGH to induce my eggs to full maturity prior to retrieval. I also realize that I have about twelve new mosquito bites. Low season, my foot. I hop to the door while scratching my leg and discover to my astonishment that it's Abhi on the other side. Since when does Abhi knock? Then I realize, it must be because of Alex. He doesn't walk into another man's room unannounced, the way he regularly walked into mine. This seems both bizarre and a little frustrating. Why is Alex's privacy more important than mine? Why are there different cultural boundaries for him than there are for me?

"Morning, Aidren, I have good news," says Abhi. "Dr. Patel says chu and Alex will come please to the clinic to see Vaina."

"Now?" I say, looking at Alex, who is still fast asleep and snoring. We had asked Dr. Patel the day before if she could arrange for Alex to be able to meet Vaina, but we had thought it would take some time. I had hoped that we could sleep in today and take advantage of the fact that there is no morning shot on this final day of IVF. No such luck. But my heart skips at the thought of Alex's meeting Vaina. It's another moment I have been looking forward to for a long time.

"Okay, we'll be down in a few minutes, thank you, Abhi." I go to rouse my slumbering husband. Half an hour later, we are freshly showered, dressed, and on our way to the clinic. When we arrive, we are led to the small meeting room where I first met Vaina. As we pass the semen collection room, I think I see Alex flinch. PTSD.

We enter the meeting room and Vaina is sitting there, her hair glossy and oiled, her black eyes glistening, though again cast down.

"Good morning, Vaina. This is my husband, Alex," I say, and she smiles and I giggle. We laugh a lot and this makes me happy as it is only the second time we have met. I think it might be because we are both at a loss for words. But also, people in general laugh a lot in India. I sort of like it, and I find it easy to fall into this rhythm. Sometimes a giggle says so much more than words ever can.

"It's so nice to meet you," says Alex, who looks uncharacteristically unsettled and at a loss for words at the sight of Vaina. Seeing Vaina, the woman who will hopefully carry our child and

bring him or her into the world, has brought home the stark re-
alities of this process. I recognize the look on his face. It's India
sneaking up on him. It's nice to know that I'm not alone.

"Thank you so much for what you are doing for us. We are so
grateful," says Alex, with an earnest, boyish smile on his face. He
is terribly nervous. The translator, Ayisha, motions for him to
take a seat in the chair by Vaina, which he does. Ayisha tells
Vaina what Alex has just said. His eyes, just like mine, dart back
and forth between the two women, trying not to miss a thing.

Vaina smiles, and holds Alex's hand for a moment and looks
into my eyes and then into his. "I am so happy to do this for you
and Atrine, because I want you to have what I have, a happy,
healthy family."

My husband has only cried three times in his life. Once,
when his childhood dog Spoogoo,* who was quite literally his
best friend, died. The second time was when we lost Colette; I
had never seen him break down in this way ever before, but it
brought us so much closer. The third time is today. I am so accustomed to Alex's being the rational, almost stoic one, while I
am the emotional one. The translator and I look at each other,
both of us a bit uncomfortable, but Vaina looks completely
sympathetic and at ease. It's as if she understands instinctively
what Alex is feeling. She squeezes Alex's hand in hers and
smiles. I can see her eyes fill up with tears also, which of course
turns on my waterworks, no surprise on that front. And then, as
quickly as it began, our meeting ends.

I hug Vaina good-bye, and we hold on to each other for a long
time. We both know that this is probably going to be the last
time we see each other until I return for the birth, if we are

---

* A family pet name. Jenny's father had been an ophthalmologist in Africa, and
the local word for eye doctor was something approaching "spoogoo."

lucky enough to get to that point. Yet somehow, after just two brief visits, I feel connected to her in a way that I never would have imagined. Despite our differences in language, culture, age, and experience, there is already a thread that we're both reluctant to break.

❀❀❀

That night, as we settle in to wait for the final shot before my egg retrieval in the morning, Alex and I try to talk through the emotions of the afternoon. Every moment since he arrived here has felt so charged.

"Today, when I met Vaina, I was overwhelmed with a sense of gratitude. This woman is willing to do something for us that we are unable to do for ourselves. I'll never know or understand what Vaina's reasons for doing this truly are. I suspect like in life, there are many reasons and motivations. There is never just one simple answer. But whatever the reasons, I just feel so grateful and so happy right now." Alex's voice breaks with heavy emotion, and I grab his hand tightly in mine. As the sun sinks over the minaret outside our window, the evening prayers rise from the twilight. It feels like India is putting her arms around us and wishing us sweet dreams.

At the stroke of midnight, there's a knock on the door. I open the door to see one of the ubiquitous nurses in a sari. I let her in, at which point, I notice she has brought a very long needle with her. And then, just as deftly and suddenly as these things come upon you at the clinic, before I have any chance to poise myself for the pain, she plunges the needle in my left thigh. Then, as quickly as she has entered, the nurse leaves, with a soft smile and a barely audible *namaste*; her work here is done. I try to smile, but it comes out more like a grimace. The beesting metaphor has been a vast understatement. I feel like someone is holding me down with force while hundreds of bees sting me all over my body.

Alex can tell that I'm in agony. Maybe it's the fact that I'm lying on the bed with my eyes closed, breathing slowly and gripping the bedspread with a white-knuckled vise grip. Or maybe it's all the terrible jokes he's telling, in hopes of distracting me with laughter. After all those days of missing my husband, right now I just want to pretend he isn't here.

"Please, don't talk to me for a sec," I manage to force out, "I just need to lie here, in peace." I try to remember every bit of yoga I've ever learned: breathe deeply into the core, center my thoughts, focus on the now. Oh, who am I kidding? This *hurts*.

"What can I do for you?" Alex asks, rushing to prop a pillow under my head. At this moment, I could ask for the moon and the stars and Alex would actually try to bring them to me. Breathe in, breathe out.

"Well," I say, when I finally regain enough composure to speak, "at least I didn't punch you in the eye."

"What?"

"I need a Coke," I say, "and is there a bag of Ruffles around?"

Not quite the moon and the stars, but at midnight in Anand, it might just as well have been. Valiant Alex is somehow able to chase down the much-needed sugars, salt, and fats. Egg retrieval is tomorrow, so I'm not allowed to eat or drink anything after 1:00 a.m.—easier said than done, since I feel like I've eaten everything in sight upon arriving here—and miraculously, Alex returns with the treats before lockdown. It is one of the most amazing acts of love he has ever performed for me.

❊❈❊

When Abhi knocks on the door the next morning, Alex is already in the bathroom, along with a jar that Dr. Patel reluctantly gave us when Alex announced he would never darken the doorstep of the semen collection room ever again. He comes out with the jar tucked into a neat little brown paper lunch bag and a big grin on his face.

"One of these little fellas is about to get very lucky," he says, shaking the bag and smiling at me. I roll my eyes and pull the pillow over my head. Alex's contribution to this process has literally taken two minutes, whereas I will have to be poked and prodded under anesthesia.

Dr. Patel has explained to me in detail what will happen this morning during the egg retrieval process. A needle, which is attached to an ultrasound probe, will be inserted into my vagina. Then, using the ultrasound to locate the ovarian follicles, Dr. Patel will puncture each follicle and carefully remove the egg and the fluid within the follicle. Then the eggs will be placed in a culture dish, combined with Alex's sperm, and placed in an incubator to wait for fertilization. I know that I will be under general anesthesia during today's procedure, but as I think over the nitty-gritty of egg retrieval, I'm not sure I'm ready for what comes next.

Abhi knocks again, this time with more urgency. *This is it, the morning you've been waiting for, so get up and let's go get this over with!* The pep talk at least gets me out of bed and into the shower. I feel nervous, of course, but I also feel a little excitement mixed with dread—bigger needles!—and relief too. At the very least, the daily IVF shots are finally going to be over, and soon, Alex and I can go home. Life will go on as normal. I choke on a laugh. Normal? What does that even *mean* anymore?

Abhi is waiting for us downstairs looking chagrined. We are running a bit late for our appointment, but even worse, today, the only vehicles Abhi has available are two mopeds. *Of all mornings*, I think as I climb onto the back of the first moped behind a friend of Abhi's who will serve as my moped chauffeur. Before I figure out where exactly I should hold on, the driver guns the engine and we dart into the busy flow of traffic. I look behind me and catch a glimpse of Alex and Abhi, perched on the other moped. Alex is holding on to Abhi with one hand, clutching his precious brown paper lunch sack with the other, trying desperately not to drop it. I realize that, as Jenny promised, this is one of those snapshots from this adventure that I will never forget. Watching my husband try to stay on the moped while saving both his sample and his dignity is absolutely priceless. Alex is never, *ever* going to live this one down.

We arrive at the clinic—Alex, myself, and the precious sample—all intact. I check in with the nurses, and even though I've been looking forward to this day, right now I am becoming a ball of nervous energy. *Hungry* nervous energy. Alex kisses me and holds me close for a long time; he tells me that everything is going to be okay, and I actually begin to believe him. All too soon, it is time. Alex is led to a waiting area, and I am put on a gurney and wheeled into the operating room.

This is not like any operating room I have ever seen before. There is no sterile metal table, no high-tech equipment beeping in the background, no bright overhead lights, and no privacy. In fact, there is a woman undergoing a procedure just a few yards away, and I can hear Dr. Patel calling for clamps and suction. At that moment I have a terrible feeling of claustrophobia. My first impulse is to jump off the bed and run fast and far, but I have come too far to stop now, haven't I? My imagination is going wild, but I decide if I die from a botched procedure, then at least I did it in pursuit of a noble cause. But make no mistake, I am terrified, but containing the panic . . . barely.

I squeeze my eyes shut, and when I open them, I see an entire team of masked doctors and nurses heading toward me, gloved hands outstretched. This robed and rubber-gloved battalion seems like an army sent from some pulp slasher movie. Suddenly, and for really the first time, the clinic feels very foreign, and at that given moment everything feels wrong, unsettling, and dirty to me. I see Dr. Patel, and just the fact that I recognize one of the masked faces makes me feel a bit better. But not much. I think I'm going to have an anxiety attack.

"Please put me under," I hiss to Dr. Patel. "I don't want to be conscious anymore!"

I wake up about a half hour later in a recovery room with Alex at my side, holding my hand. It's all over.

"You did great," says Alex, kissing my forehead.

I grip his hand tightly. After all this effort, what if the egg retrieval didn't go well? Dr. Patel walks through the door, still in her surgical cap and sari, and I hold my breath. She squeezes my hand gently.

"Everything went very well, good job, Adrienne. You're feeling all right?"

I release Alex's hand, just enough so that the blood can begin to flow again, and exhale a sigh of relief. "Yes, fine. Hungry." I smile.

"Well, you still have the hormones in your system, but that will pass soon and you will return to your normal appetite. We will do the fertilization and implantation the day after tomorrow, and in two weeks, we will know if the IVF has been successful. Enjoy the rest of your stay, and have a safe trip home." And then, as abruptly as she entered our lives, Dr. Patel is gone, disappearing into the crowd of nurses, surrogates, and genetic couples, all of them looking to her to make their fragile dreams into a reality.

❊☙❊☙❊

The next day, Alex and I leave Anand for good. We're headed to Rajasthan for a little sightseeing of palaces and fortresses, and from there, we will travel on to Mumbai, before heading home. As we climb into Abhi's car for perhaps the last time, I think about Vaina. She is undergoing implantation at this very moment. Is she frightened, as I was yesterday? Is she alone? In that instant, I wish more than anything that I were by her side. I wouldn't be able to be in the operating room with her, so I wouldn't be able to do much for her but sit in the waiting room, but perhaps it would have helped put her mind at ease. I will my spirit into the medical room with her, to comfort her from afar and, in the loosest sense, hold her hand.

The trip to Rajasthan is wonderful. Alex and I wander the streets, soaking in the local flavor, and luxuriate in the amenities of our first four-star hotel. Mostly, we try to enjoy each other's company and distract ourselves from what might or might not be happening with Vaina. We've been disappointed too many times to let ourselves anticipate anything. We resolve to be patient, to see what comes, and to know, whether the IVF has been successful or not, that we will be okay, because we are together.

Two days later, as we leave Mumbai, I hold Alex's hand and think of the day I met Vaina, sitting peacefully in the middle of a sunbeam in that little room, smiling at me. And for the first time in a long time, I begin to expect the best.

chapter 7

I'm sitting at a Dean & Deluca on Lexington Avenue sipping a latte and staring at my iPhone. *Come on, vibrate!* Somebody at the next table gives me a look; have I actually yelled this out loud? New Yorkers have a very high threshold for public acts of insanity, but that doesn't mean I want to become the lady who yells at inanimate objects. I pull out my laptop and start to work on nothing, pretending to be sane, which of course, I'm totally not. I'm crazy with anticipation.

It's been two weeks since Alex and I left India; two long weeks of waiting and wondering and trying not to get excited but getting way too excited anyway, followed by periods of dread that all of this will have been for naught. I think about having to go through IVF all over again. I think about giving up. The doldrums hit. The doldrums recede. I shop. I work. I wait. I worry.

❊❊❊❊❊

When I was pregnant, there was a gentle evolution toward changing our lives and having a child. There were doctor appointments to attend, test results to fret over, new clothes to buy, schedules to plan. There was a rhythm. What struck Alex and me both about doing a surrogacy overseas was how removed we were from everything that was happening.

When Alex and I made the decision to select surrogacy abroad, one of the things we asked ourselves was if it was going to be weird for us to be in the United States, while our surrogate was pregnant with our child in India. This was a stumbling block for both of us. At the time we made the decision, I thought it would be less difficult to have a surrogate far away. If she were close by, I know I would be checking in on her every day. Distance, as problematic as it might be, would force me to respect her boundaries. But now, two weeks after leaving Anand, I am desperate for information and frustrated that I am so far away from the events that will so dramatically change my life. I feel very disconnected, not part of this process. Alex describes it as sharp shocks of events, followed by a long period of nothing with no word, no updates. It's driving us crazy.

At the clinic, the surrogates are in good hands, with their health constantly supervised. There is a chef at the surrogate house who prepares balanced meals filled with all the necessary vitamins, nutrients, and calories pregnant women need. The surrogates take part in daily classes, have regular medical checkups, and generally have access to anything and everything they need to be healthy and safe. When Alex and I were considering clinics abroad, this part of the program at Akanksha was important to us and a critical part of what we based our decision on.

When I told my father, a prominent doctor, about our decision to try surrogacy, he was supportive, thankfully, but he urged me to learn more about it both in the United States and abroad. Surrogacy is not a simple way to have a child. The process and surrounding issues are complex, and, as I'm discovering, so too are the emotions. No matter how well you may have prepared, when things start to play out, it's not always the way you were expecting them to.

Today is the day that we are supposed to hear whether or not we're pregnant. Actually, yesterday was the day, which is why I had pushed off a business trip to New York until today. But Dr. Patel is operating on Akanksha time, meaning that nothing is done quite on the schedule it's supposed to. So, rather than be with Alex, nervously awaiting Dr. Patel's call, I am a country's breadth away from my husband, staring at my phone, desperate to find out if a woman a continent away is carrying our baby. (Did you follow that? I barely did.)

My iPhone vibrates. I jump out of the chair with a shriek. It's an email from the clinic. I squint at the letters on my screen trying to make sense of the simple message, but the waves of adrenaline now coursing through my veins have turned the letters into characters as meaningless as hieroglyphics. I breathe deeply, try an *ohm*, and look again: *Congratulations, you have a positive result!*

I shriek again and immediately dial Alex. The guy at the table next to me moves to the opposite end of the café. I can't blame him. I am definitely the crazy lady in the café right now, and it feels *fabulous*.

"Alex!" I say breathlessly the second he picks up the phone. "Vaina is pregnant. We're going to have a baby!"

Alex audibly exhales and then he says, "Really?! My love—this is so wonderful. Oh, Adrienne, I can't believe it. We did it!"

"I love you," I cry, "I'll be on the next flight home, and we'll celebrate together." I hang up and let Alex's magical words envelop me. *We did it.* We are finally, miraculously, going to become parents. I feel instantly calm. Nothing can faze me now. I'm floating in a warm and tranquil sea beneath a pastel pink and blue sky.

❀❀❀❀

My moment of serenity is short-lived. Are we having a boy or a girl? For parents having babies the old-fashioned way, gender can be determined as early as twelve weeks. With in vitro fertilization, because fully formed embryos are placed into the womb, it is possible to know the gender of these embryos before implantation. I know that here in the States, it is possible to direct your doctor to implant only male or female embryos, but Dr. Patel does not allow such engineering.

I somehow lasted four weeks without knowing whether or not Vaina was pregnant, but eventually I reach the point where I can't wait another second without knowing if I will have a daughter or a son. I have to know *now*. I email the clinic immediately and impatiently wait for a response. It's two in the morning in India, so realistically, any response won't come for hours, if ever. I have a vague memory that the clinic has a policy about not revealing the sex of the baby. Maybe Dr. Patel is afraid that genetic parents will back out if they don't get their gender of choice, but Alex and I would be overjoyed no matter what. We, like most parents, just hope for ten fingers and ten toes. But how on earth can I wait nine months to find out? Breathe in. Breathe out. Breath in....

Thirty hours later, Alex and I are at our favorite sushi joint toasting our future together as a family. Sushi was a passion I had to forgo when I was pregnant, so our meal is one of the unexpected blessings of surrogacy—I can have my sushi and my baby too. It doesn't quite make up for the experience of carrying my own child, but I'm taking my tender mercies where I can find them. Dr. Patel still hasn't responded to my email, but I'm trying not to think about that. In these first wonderful moments as a new family, Alex and I are doing our best to focus exclusively on the sheer joy we are feeling. But neither one of us can resist guessing.

"Do you want a boy or girl?" Alex asks a little sheepishly. "I mean, not that it matters, I know we'll be happy with either."

"Either would be fine with me too," I say, "although it would be helpful to know who I'm shopping for."

"I think secretly you're hoping for a girl," says Alex, smiling teasingly. "Boys are messy and they break things. You're too much of a neat freak for a boy."

"Yeah, yeah—whatever." I punch him lightly in the arm. "I think you're secretly hoping for a boy. I would love a little boy who looks like you. I can be messy too, you know." Alex looks at me skeptically. He knows that I have never been messy one single day in my life, but this is a new life now, and I'm willing to be flexible. "Well, I *could.* For our son, I could become an absolute slob. You wait and see."

"All I care about is that he or she can play soccer, so I can be the coach. Boy or girl, they just have to be able to come out and play with his or her old man and kick it down the field. So if it's a girl, you can't make our princess wear dresses *all* the time. And if it's a boy, keep a lid on the linen trousers every once in a while, so that we can go out and get messy. Deal?"

"Deal!" Alex and I laugh and raise our sake glasses and toast our unbelievably good fortune. Another tender mercy, sake during pregnancy. Of course, this time I'm not the pregnant one, but isn't this still my pregnancy? We'd only been pregnant for one day and already things were starting to get a little confusing. But I've never been one to let a few mixed emotions get in the way of a celebration, or a glass of good sake. Alex and I toast the pregnancy, then we toast each other, and then, we toast our baby boy or girl who is growing inside Vaina, half a world away.

On the way home, blissfully warm and a bit tipsy from all the sake, we start brainstorming names. I mention lots of Indian-inspired, Hindu and Sanskrit names, which I'd been manically researching for the last two weeks while trying to deal with the waiting game. In my family, it's a tradition to give children a name that begins with the letter *A*, and with Alex by my side, I'm sure he could be convinced to follow the Arieff tradition. I fall asleep that night dreaming of boys' and girls' names that begin with *A*. Andrea, Avery, Ariel, Anthony, Alexis, Artemis...Artemis? I wake with a start in the middle of the night. I need to talk to Dr. Patel.

It is the middle of the day in Anand, so the chances that I will catch her are small, but somehow, I am put straight through. She answers in her typical assured, professional manner, and for a moment, I am transported to balmy Anand. "Dr. Patel! It's Adrienne Arieff. Alex and I are so happy that Vaina is pregnant. It's really phenomenal news, and I know I'm not supposed to ask you this, but can you tell me if we are having a boy or girl?"

"It's two girls," she says brusquely. And then she hangs up.

I have never been so delighted to have someone hang up on me in all my life. Girls! "Alex, wake up," I say, shaking my husband awake while giggling uncontrollably. "Wake up! I just talked to Dr. Patel. We're having two girls! Wait, *two* girls? Is that what she said? *Two* girls?" I'm thrilled, but maybe I misunderstood Dr. Patel? I must have misheard her. Or could she have made a mistake?

"What? Adrienne, what's happening?" says Alex, slowly arriving at consciousness, struggling valiantly to keep up with me.

"I spoke to Dr. Patel, and I think she said that we are having two girls."

"Two? You think? You didn't clarify this with her?" Alex

asks. It may be three in the morning, but I told you, he's a lawyer.

"She didn't give me a chance. The clinic has a rule about revealing the sex of the babies, so she only told me on the sly, and she hung up before I could really say anything. I'm pretty sure she said two girls."

"Well," says Alex pragmatically, "at least they're both girls, which cuts the list of possible names in half."

"And doubles the lists for everything else," I say, trying to wrap my mind around this incredible news. Alex and I had always intended to have one baby. One child was something you could plan for, something that would bring us joy and round out our family of two into a family of three. We, as adults, would always outnumber the kids. But two babies? That didn't sound quite so easy. Two girls. We are going to be the parents of *two girls*. How unexpected but amazingly wonderful is that?

"Alex," I say, realizing it for the first time, "we're going to have *twins*!"

Alex and I laugh and rejoice in our good fortune. This is astonishing news, and I must fight the urge to call everyone I know and love. I had wanted to know the gender of the baby—*babies*—so I could better focus on preparing our life and our home for their arrival. As I lie back down next to my sleeping husband, I'm realizing that now that I can picture the pink booties and the little feet that go inside them, I'm suddenly seized with debilitating anxiety. What if Vaina loses this pregnancy? What if our twins meet the same fate as sweet Colette?

I try to picture Vaina in my mind, resting each day on her bed, surrounded by the other women in the surrogate house. I visualize her relaxing, feeling calm and peaceful, eating healthfully, and receiving good medical treatment. I imagine her

planning the nursing classes she wants to take with the surrogacy fee we're paying her. I imagine her healthy, and happy, and
safe.

But I'm so far away I can only imagine.

As time passes, we tell people slowly, as we begin to feel comfortable. Our family and friends are, for the most part, supportive of our choice. I do find myself answering pointed questions
from some skeptics: *Don't you think you are exploiting this poor
woman in India? Do you think it's safe? Did you just not want to deal
with being pregnant?* And, my favorite, the question I told Alex
would raise its ugly head: *Oh, so you don't have to gain weight now?!*
A few people asked me if I'd ever read *The Handmaid's Tale*, a
dystopian novel by Margaret Atwood in which fertile young
women are enslaved as reproductive servants.

At times, I just want to scream, *This isn't like opting for takeout
because I don't feel like cooking! I've had three miscarriages! I can't
carry a child. I would have carried my own baby if I could.* The friends
who suggest that I chose surrogacy because I didn't want to get
fat clearly do not understand how painful those losses were for
me and what a toll they took on my body and my marriage.
But for those who are asking the deeper questions, who believe
that I am exploiting Vaina by going to India, I return their
questions with a few of my own. Who do they think volunteers
for surrogacy in the United States? Are *those* women being ex-
ploited? Why do they think that they know what is right for
Vaina better than she does? And why do they believe that Vaina
is not free to make her own choices about her own body?

With my second miscarriage, I went through a similar heartbreak, but I also began to question myself and life itself. Was I
even supposed to have kids? Was I inferior because I couldn't
carry a baby? Was this nature's way of telling me I was making
a mistake? I deeply insecure and hypersensitive to everything,

I began to believe that my friends were editing their conversations about their own kids in order to spare my feelings. Then, with the third miscarriage, I was just over it. I wouldn't talk to anybody but Alex about what I was feeling, and mostly what I was feeling was that I was done. Done with the blood, and the cramping, and the heartbreaking loss.

But now, I wasn't done anymore. My heart was once again open and vulnerable. Thankfully, an overwhelming majority of the people we've shared our news with are happy for us and tell us that this is an incredible gift. They believe that our story is inspiring. The haters have had their effect, sadly, and I am still hesitant about telling the world that we are expecting. For those who do not know the sad struggles of the past, our acquaintances, colleagues, and casual friends, I tell them that we had fertility challenges and chose surrogacy. End of story. I struggle to be honest and straightforward and, most important, not to be embarrassed by our choice. I am proud of our actions, though that doesn't mean I want to open a discussion about something so sensitive and deeply personal.

I spend a lot of time thinking about my relationship with Vaina. What is a good relationship with your surrogate supposed to look like? Are we friends? Are we business partners? We are involved in a deal of sorts, and I want it to be a win-win for both of us. At least, I hope that's the way she'll feel about this, but how could I possibly know, when we can't understand each other's language?

I have several friends around my age who are pregnant with their first child while Vaina is pregnant with mine. I was not a woman who loved being pregnant, but when I see them, I miss the feeling of a baby growing inside me. I miss that connection that only a mother can have with a child when it is within her body, when that baby is wholly reliant on its mother to feed, shelter, and protect it. This is the experience that Vaina is now having with my daughters. I try hard to remember that I am not a failure. Alex and I have only come to this place in our journey after being through death and sorrow. Knowing that our babies are growing in Vaina's womb is beyond fulfilling. Yet, it is a double-edged sword.

I want to feel close to Vaina, to remain connected indefinitely, even after the birth. But how are we going to develop a bond when I'm here and she's there? We can't even exchange letters because neither Vaina nor her husband can read or write. So how will she know that I'm thinking of her, caring about her, even if from a distance? I want to do whatever I can to help her, to empower her. I know that the amount of money that she will receive from carrying my children is more money than she will ever have had at one time in her entire life, and probably more than she'll ever have again unless she decides to do another surrogacy with another couple.

I know through Dr. Patel that Vaina was not able to complete much school before she became a wife and mother herself. I want the best for her children. I want to make sure they can get access to an education. The surrogacy fee could take care of this.

I didn't expect to feel so much for Vaina or for her family, especially since I've met her only a handful of times. I wonder if other moms feel like this about their surrogates, if they too want to develop a closer relationship. From what I've read, most surrogates have the baby and then return to their families, never to be seen or heard from again. That's it. It's similar to a closed adoption. This was initially attractive to me, but now it feels uncomfortable and unnatural. I suddenly wish Alyssa, Caroline, or one of the other genetic moms I met in Anand were here to talk about this with me. I need somebody who understands, who has been through this, to tell me how I'm supposed to feel.

❀❀❀❀

The radio silence from India wears on me—patience is a virtue that I have done without—and it is beginning to get Alex too. Part of this, I think, is cultural. From our doctor's perspective, all we can do is to wait, be patient, and let nature take its course. We, of course, want weekly updates, up-to-the-minute ultrasounds, and postcards reporting on every kick. Our expectations are apparently profoundly misplaced. But this doesn't stop us from wanting news. I write to Dr. Patel on a nearly daily basis, and Alex chides me for it. Dr. Patel probably does too, but with a continent and an ocean between us, I never hear her complaints. Instead, she just doesn't answer me. I hear nothing but deafening silence.

"Adrienne, don't write her *again,*" says Alex, when he catches me sneaking in yet another nudge note.

"I can't help it!" I say, and it's true. I can't stop myself, I'm dying for news, just a paragraph, two sentences, three words, anything! What I would really love is a picture of Vaina pregnant, so that I can see for myself that this is really true, that we're really having a baby—correction, *babies*—and that I am somehow connected to this pregnancy. "I promise, it's a nice email. Just listen: *Dear Dr. Patel, I know that you're busy but it would mean a lot if you could just take a few seconds out of your day to drop me a line about how Vaina is doing, and maybe even send me a picture. Alex and I are so excited at this news, but we haven't heard a word from you for weeks, and we would like to be updated. Please respond soonest.*"

"Adrienne, don't yell at Dr. Patel," says Alex, and comes up behind me, wrapping his arms around my shoulders, giving me a comforting hug, while also surreptitiously moving my hands well clear of the send button.

"I'm not yelling; I'm just *asking*. It's different. I was nice!"

"Listen, Adrienne, there's nothing we can do at this point but trust Dr. Patel and Vaina and the process. You have to come to terms with that, or you're going to drive me, your family, most of your friends, Dr. Patel, and, most importantly, yourself, absolutely insane."

I know that he's right. Alex is usually right. I don't send this particular email, but I know I will send others, when Alex isn't looking. I try my very best to be patient. I bury myself in work. I shop. I read. I do yoga probably more than is good for me. Yes, it turns out you really can overdose on Zen.

Finally, and just when I least expect it, Dr. Patel answers my prayers and sends me a picture of Vaina, who shows a small, but distinct, baby bump. It's everything I could hope for. She is at a Krishna shower that the other surrogates and Dr. Patel threw for her at around week 22. She's dressed in a beautiful red sari, and surrounded by flowers and prayers and song. She looks exactly as I have been imagining her—calm, peaceful, happy, well cared for, and very definitely pregnant.

"Alex!" I shriek when the image materializes on my screen. "Vaina is pregnant!"

"Yes, Adrienne, I know." Alex is getting used to humoring me on this subject. I don't think he even hears me anymore. I think he believes that this is the surrogacy version of craving pickles and ice cream. Not a moment to argue; just nod and agree with the obvious.

"No, look! We got a picture, and Vaina looks *pregnant*. And really happy. Oh, Alex, she looks so great!"

This gets his attention. He snaps out of his indulgent-husband coma and is behind me, gazing into the screen, in two seconds flat. We are there for a long time, just staring, not saying a thing. I smile brightly and broadly and soon, I start to giggle. I cannot believe that this wonderful thing is actually, truly, happening. Alex joins me and we start to giggle like two little kids. Before we know it, we're hugging each other and jumping up and down. Despite all the dread and disconnection we've gone through in this process, we allow ourselves to revel in this moment, nothing short of ecstatic.

Over the next few weeks I start to talk to my friends more substantively about the twins coming. Now that I have seen Vaina pregnant, I feel more comfortable. I still get some weird questions when I mention our Indian surrogate, like, Will the babies be brown because they are being carried by an Indian woman? Doesn't anybody take biology in high school anymore? The worst is when I send the photo of Vaina out to some close friends and a few comment that she doesn't look very pregnant and am I sure the babies are okay?

I'm finding it a little hard to confine our news to my elevator pitch anymore. I find myself lapsing into lengthy monologues on the subject of foreign gestational surgery and, worse, defending our choice, and explaining to people why we aren't violating any medical or social ethical codes. Still, I don't feel that I have anything to "defend." It was a choice that Alex, Vaina, and I all made willingly, and there's no reason for anyone to call our motivations or actions into question, and I am constantly educating everyone I know about every minute detail.

It can get emotionally and mentally exhausting. I have decided that when my adventure is over, I'm going to do my best to try and educate people about the process. I believe more firmly than ever that each couple should be granted the respect and privacy to make the fertility choice that is right for them. I decide that I want to prepare genetic moms who choose surrogacy for the barrage of questions they might face, and reassure them that it is possible to navigate this process in a way that feels positive, and very right.

At twenty-two weeks we get our second sonogram picture. We're beyond thrilled to receive it, and stare at it for hours trying to feel something about the image, but to be honest, it's hard. Colette's sonogram was so clear, and we formed an instant bond with her. She had a face and fingers and even a smile, and as we watched her move and flip on the screen, we saw a budding personality. We could tell how gorgeous she was, and that she was a happy spirit. This sonogram picture looks more like two fuzzy white blobs floating in space. The blobs don't look like Colette; they don't even look like fetuses. I don't feel a connection to these images at all, which terrifies me. I expected to feel a rush of love for these babies—*my* babies—and instead, I feel absolutely nothing. For the first time, I start to wonder if I should just drop everything and go back to India. I want desperately to be by Vaina's side, close to the pregnancy—close to my developing babies. I want to feel the bond with them that I felt with Colette.

My sister and my best girlfriends arrange showers for me in San Francisco and New York City. They call the parties "a celebration of the birth of Adrienne's twins." I like the way that this phrase sums things up without being too specific. I'm too superstitious after Colette to call this a "baby shower."

Both events are wonderful. All the friends whom I depend on at every critical juncture in my life are there, with broad smiles, beautifully wrapped gifts, and their own stories of motherhood, to help me focus on the joy and blessings that are about to enter our lives.

I'm surrounded by love and songs and prayers, and women in beautiful dresses, just like Vaina at her Krishna shower. I should be feeling happy and peaceful, loved and celebrated... but I'm not. I'm brooding and distracted. To be honest, I'm a little bit of a party pooper. I don't want to be—these women have done such a wonderful thing for me—but I can tell I'm a wet blanket.

I get great gifts. I eat a lot of cake, everybody hugs me. But I'm not there. In my mind, I'm in India, by Vaina's side, waiting calmly and peacefully for the birth of my babies.

"Adrienne," says my friend Maja, bringing me back to reality. "Are you okay?"

"Yes, I'm sorry I'm distracted," I say. I feel bad. My friends have gone to so much trouble to make this special occasion for me, and I can't even concentrate.

"No worries," says Maja, who always understands. "After all, it's your party, and you can cry if you want to. We all understand. There's a lot going on."

"That's just it," I say. "There's so much going on, and it's all going on a million miles away. Meanwhile, nothing is going on here, and I'm crawling the walls."

"Well," says Nicole, who comes in mid-conversation and cuts right to the chase as usual. "If that's how you feel, why don't you get yourself on a plane and go to India and see her? It's not like you don't have the frequent flyer miles. For God's sake, Adrienne, stop driving us all crazy and go to India already, honey."

Suddenly I feel like a thousand pounds had been lifted off my shoulders. I can concentrate again. I can experience the joy in the festivities and take comfort from the company of my friends and family. I can celebrate the pregnancy the way I should, because I know I am going to go home and tell Alex that I have to go to India, that that's where I belong right now.

✳︎❧✳︎❧

"*Hi, my love,*" says Alex, smiling with amusement as I walk through the door, my arms loaded down with trinkets, grinning from ear to ear. "Looks like you had fun, and cleaned up in the baby accessory department. These are going to be the best-dressed girls in San Francisco...although I don't see any soccer jerseys in here."

"Alex," I say a little tentatively, "we need to talk."

"Sure, what's up?" He takes my hand and leads me to the sofa. I drop all the packages and cuddle into the crook of his arm, and then I dive in.

"Alex, I want to go back to India. I want to be with Vaina, with the girls. I know it sounds crazy, but I just can't concentrate here. The waiting is killing me, I feel so disconnected from everything. I want to be a part of this. I can work from there just as easily. Do you understand?"

"Of course I understand," says Alex. "But unfortunately, you'll have to go alone. There is no way I can get away from the office right now. How long do you think you want to be away?"

"I don't know," I say, realizing I hadn't considered this. "I'll have to see when I get there. Maybe just seeing Vaina will make me feel better. Or," I say, knowing that what I am about to say is more likely, "maybe I'll stay until the babies are born."

"Well, we'll play it by ear, then, just like we have done all along. That seems to be working pretty well for us," Alex says, and hugs me closer. "Now, let's get some rest. Tomorrow's a big day. We've got lots of arrangements to make."

And just like that, I fall asleep and have India in my mind.

I'm in the clinic, caring for Vaina, bringing her fruit and chocolate. We're laughing at nothing, and when it gets very hot, I fan her. Mostly we just sit quietly together, not saying much, but it doesn't really matter. We just sit quietly, while Vaina's children play at her feet, and wait for my girls to be born.

chapter 8

I have always been attracted to chaos. In fact, I thrive on it. I'm infatuated with change, with unfamiliar places and cultures. I'm magnetically drawn to risk; rather than running from the unknown, I run toward it, full speed ahead. I've always liked this about myself—I've always wanted to be different—and I want my girls to be different too. Because of the route we have chosen for them to enter the world, I know that they will be. I am very happy about this, and happy to be there when their unique journey begins, in India.

India is a fascinating and dynamic place, especially right now. Alex says it reminds him of what the United States must have been like a decade after the industrial revolution. The country is in transition and it feels like it is up for anything and everything. Change is in the air and there is an exhilarating and vibrant quality to everything.

From the minute I step onto the street in the city of Ahmedabad, just two hours way from Anand and yet worlds apart, I am submerged in a tidal wave of color, everywhere, a blaze of heat, dust, people and stalls filled with mangoes, watermelon, bananas, flowers—jasmine, marigolds, roses—spices, and incense everywhere. Outdoor markets are organized by commodity, so down one side street is nothing but clothes for sale, another fruit, another spice, and down yet another, religious sculptures, pottery, and handcrafts abound. India assails all the senses. I can't think about anything beyond taking in the flavors and smells and the sounds of religious chanting at all hours from sunrise to sunset.

The textiles here are gorgeous, finely crafted, and ubiquitous—silks, cottons, and wools, Varanasi brocades, Ikat clothing, pashmina shawls, and Rajasthani mirrored and embroidered cotton. Westerners come here to these markets to buy fabric and have tailors make clothes for close to nothing, which is what I do also, since it is so hot out here and Indian cotton is the only fabric that can breathe in heat that regularly soars to 115 degrees.

There is much that I had forgotten about this place in the time I was home, but something I can never forget is the traffic. You don't hit the road here, you join an ever-flowing current of vehicles—cars, motorcycles, rickshaws, donkeys—and where you end up has more to do with the direction of the current than your own agenda. Sometimes there are so many people blowing their horns at once that I have to cover my ears. They say here that there are three kinds of cities in India: bad, very bad, and Ahmedabad!

There is tourism in the larger cities, but in Anand, and even here in Ahmedabad, which is a major city in the region but is still very much holding on to its traditions, tourists are scarce. The people shopping the market today range from suave, polo-playing upper-class society types to turbaned rickshaw or camel drivers. Yet, no matter their station in life, you do feel a fierce national pride from the people here.

The acrid smell of food frying hits you like a wall. The people I see buying food from these food stalls are never Westerners, as the newspapers in India regularly warn tourists not to buy food at stalls because, unless you are used to the local microbes, this food can actually kill you. Two children died yesterday from eating a slushie; the vendor used so much expired food coloring that they immediately started vomiting and then, tragically, died. India is not for the faint of heart.

These things happen in India. No matter where you go, you can't avoid the poverty. It's everywhere, right up against some of the greatest treasures of the world. India is a country of great diversity. The economy is growing here at breakneck speed, and there is a burgeoning middle class of workers who make their livelihoods in call centers and medical services. But, despite being the largest democracy in the world, much of life here in Anand continues to be governed by ancestral customs and the lingering effects of the caste system. There is no social safety net in India. The poverty is startling. There are rats running along the streets, whole families sleeping on torn boxes by the side of the road. Even as India develops quickly into a global power and one of the world's largest economies, millions of Indians live in circumstances that are virtually unchanged from those of their parents, grandparents, and generations before.

As I look out over the sea of colliding contrast that fills the streets here, I remember that I came to India five years ago to cleanse my soul and purify my spirit following a death. Now I am back, to help usher in life.

Being back in India at last, I feel accountable, responsible, and exhilarated at the thought of motherhood. It's an odd feeling, navigating through such an important moment in my life with no road map and no guide. I feel lots of anxiety, mixed with anticipation and incredible excitement. The chaos of India seems somehow to go with all the chaos of starting a family—it seems like a perfect marriage, and I'm so glad that I'm here.

I have always felt independent, self-sufficient, and secure when I'm on my own. If I had chosen to do surrogacy in California, I would have relied on others, and for some reason, with this experience, I just can't, or won't. It appeals to me to become a mom for the first time far from the advice and nagging concerns of my family and friends. I know that they would only be trying to help, but none of them has any concept of what this experience is like. I'd prefer to be surrounded by a community of genetic moms and surrogates who understand the challenges and opportunities of this path. I want to have my own experience of entering motherhood. Freedom isn't worth much if it doesn't include the freedom to make your own mistakes.

Before I left California, we called Dr. Patel to let her know I was coming. She was taken aback, although she tried not to show it. There was one of her characteristic pauses on the phone. I could almost hear her eyebrow arch. Few biological moms want to spend this much time in Anand, so far removed from their own support systems and from the comforts and familiarity of home. I, on the other hand, am eager to say a temporary farewell to my home; I *want* to be far from home. India has become, in its way, home to me now, just as Abhi said it would.

Dr. Patel has arranged for Abhi to pick me up at the airport this morning after my whirlwind tour of the sights and smells of Ahmedabad. My hotel is one of the few in the area where Abhi is not friendly with the owners, so he is forced to wait for me in the lobby, rather than barge into my room. He rushes forward with his arms outstretched and grabs my bag from my hand.

"Hello, Atrie, so good to see chu again so soon. Was it a

pleasant trip?" And then the inevitable, "And where is Mr. Alex?" Abhi looks behind me, scanning the crowd for a glimpse of my husband. Then he gets that vaguely distracted look on his face, followed immediately by an overbroad smile, which means that he disapproves but is trying not to show it. It also means that he's spied the bottle of green-label scotch that I've brought him as a present.

"Hello, Abhi, I've missed you and your wonderful laugh," I say, feeling so happy to see him that I don't even feel a twinge of my usual postfeminist annoyance about his views on solo women adventurers like myself. Abhi leads me toward the car. The second we step out of the hotel, I'm slammed with the heady heat. This time I don't feel smothered. In fact, my lungs suddenly and involuntarily expand, as I breathe in deep gulps of the glorious atmosphere of Ahmedabad. And then, for the first time in quite a long time, I exhale.

"Dr. Patel is waiting to see chu, Atria, but first we check in at the Laksh to freshen up, ches?"

"Yes," I say, and then again, "Yes!" I realize that I am actually excited about checking into a hotel with leaky plumbing, mosquitoes, and unreliable air-conditioning. I swear I even tear up remembering the unpredictable breakfast menu. Are these sympathetic pregnancy symptoms? Or am I just overjoyed to be here?

The drive from the airport to Anand is like a stroll down memory lane. I take in the convoluted streams of traffic, the beggars by the side of the road, the fireworks popping, the mellifluous prayers to Mecca undulating in the distance, and, of course, the holy cows. I greet all of these things like long-lost friends. I feel invigorated and relaxed, all at the same time. I'm not anxious, no circular obsessive thoughts. I'm not worried about anything. I am ready for whatever comes.

Abhi parks and we check in at the Hotel Laksh. In the lobby I see a fresh cluster of eager or anxious-looking couples huddling with their heads close together, talking about eggs. Surrogacy Camp is in full swing. I look for Alyssa and Caroline, but I don't see them. This is visiting time at the surrogate house, so they are most likely there. I do see one familiar face, the desk clerk, Fatima, who gives me a big hug along with my room key. We had developed a loose friendship when I was here last, and she seems to have missed me, and I realize that somehow, I've missed her too.

When I was last here, Fatima revealed to me that she lives in a slum in the rural part of Anand in a one-room hut. Her father is paralyzed and unable to work. Fatima is pretty, but so are her two sisters. Fatima has told me that she is the least pretty of the girls, so she has to work while her two sisters go to school to make them more desirable wives. So it's up to Fatima, at twenty-two years old, to support her entire family.

Her life is hard, and I feel she doesn't have a lot of happiness. In India there are so many desperate people, clinging to what little they have, that the sheer volume makes a safety net virtually impossible. The caste system may have been outlawed, but it continues to be an all-powerful cultural system here. The slums are so dismal and some of these cultural traditions so constricting, it's hard to imagine the beggars I see in the streets attaining a better life.

Even Fatima, at risk of losing her job, has asked for money from me once because she needed to buy medicine for her father. I have been told that she has begged from other guests here as well. I don't blame her. What choice does she have? She's making so little at her job, and I might have done the very same thing in her shoes. Fatima's rescue fantasy is to become a nun. She has told me that she doesn't want to marry and be abused, as her mother is. She's commented on the clinic only once. I mentioned that if she really needed money, perhaps she should consider egg donation, but she told me that she was too religious, and that God would never forgive her.

Fatima kisses me and tells me she's happy to see me and I tell her that I'm very happy to see her too. I love her beautiful face and spirit, always smiling and shining through in spite of her difficulties. The manager comes to reassure me with the usual list of completely unreliable assurances. The air-conditioner is fully functional, the toilet flushes, there are real eggs on the breakfast menu, and the mosquitoes are swarming elsewhere this time of year. (And pigs can sprout wings and fly.)

I'm not really paying attention at this point. For one thing, I was here long enough during my IVF to know that these promises will never come true. Second, I'm completely focused on going to see Vaina. I have been picturing her in my mind for months, and I can't wait to see her smile and her belly, and experience this pregnancy for the first time with something besides my imagination.

"Chu rest now. Then I will come to take chu to the clinic when Dr. Patel is finish," says Abhi, and moves toward the door to leave. But I don't want to rest. I want to see Vaina.

"Wait, can't we go now?" I say, although I know the answer to that already. I am in Anand. I am on Dr. Patel time.

"Chu will just be sitting in the lobby and waiting if you come now," says Abhi who has obviously picked up on how I feel about those plastic chairs. "Chu rest here, Atrie; I'll be back before you know it, without a doubt."

So I wait. I'm used to that. I feel as if I've been doing nothing but waiting since this adventure began. But I have to admit (despite the fact that, contrary to what the manager has told me, the room is tepid at best and I already have six mosquito bites) it is easier to wait here in Anand than in San Francisco. About eight thousand miles easier. I try to listen to Abhi's practical advice and lie down to get some rest. I know that I must be jet-lagged and exhausted, but I don't feel it. I'm running on pure expectant-mom adrenaline.

Every time I shut my eyes, I imagine myself walking into the surrogate room and seeing Vaina pregnant for the first time. I close my eyes tighter and start my version of counting sheep: mentally listing girls' names that begin with *A*: Anna, Annabelle, Anastasia, Apollonia, Avril...

I wake up to Abhi standing in the open doorway laughing and beckoning for me to hurry and get up already. Dr. Patel is ready for me.

"Come along, Atri, Dr. Patel waits for chu now."

"Okay, Abhi, hold your horses," I say scrambling out of bed, bleary-eyed, heart pounding, reaching for the touchstones of my life in India: phone, bottled water, bug spray.

As the rickshaw sways and creaks its way up to the entrance of the clinic, I am struck by the fact that it is as if no time has passed here at all. The same insouciant cows lounge in the afternoon heat, the same or a very similar family of beggars waits outside the gates, the same cheerless paint peels off the walls, the same unruffled nurses move barefoot and soundlessly from room to room with needles in their hands. This place seems frozen in time.

The nurse with the movie star smile behind the front desk gives me a hello hug and friendly wink and leads me immediately to Dr. Patel's office. *Finally,* I think, noticing how relieved I feel just being back in the clinic. The wait is over!

Dr. Patel is wearing a magnificent sari. She is a symphony of whispering peacock and midnight blue as she opens her arms to greet me. There is a string of simple but stunning pearls around her neck, and two more in each ear. Why is it that every time I see this woman she takes my breath away? I swear I think I hear myself gasp at the first sight of her. Dr. Patel is nothing short of mesmerizing.

"Hello, Adrienne, so nice to have you back so soon. How are you and your husband, Alex?"

"We're fine," I say, "we are both so excited. He's sorry he couldn't be here with me, but he couldn't get away. But I couldn't wait. I had to come."

"Yes, I could tell you were getting impatient," Dr. Patel says, and I think I hear a tiny note of disapproval whispering from between her silken pleasantries. But I can't blame her. I have been blowing up her email for months.

"Vaina will be very happy to see you. She's been asking about you every day," says Dr. Patel, offering me a chair. The arm of the chair breaks off in her hand. She puts it aside without a thought and offers me another. I sit down gingerly. I'm prone to pratfalls at moments like this, and I'm not risking it.

"She has? That's so sweet," I say, genuinely touched. "I've been thinking about her too. Can I see her now? Is she feeling okay?"

"Yes, everything is fine. Vaina has a sonogram scheduled for today, so you can go with her if you like, and see your girls. "

See my girls. I can see my girls! I should be jumping out of my chair at this news, but instead I feel overwhelmed and a bit numb.

"That's wonderful," I say. I am feeling so many things at once that I don't know which to express first. My words fall flat.

"Adrienne, I wanted to ask you a favor while you're here," Dr. Patel says, all disapproval gone, replaced by a glowing and all-knowing smile. Like I said, Nayna Patel has got it, and she knows how to use it.

"What? Oh, sure, anything," I say, still thinking about the fact that I'm going to see my babies *today* for the very first time, in person.

"Since the babies are not born and you are here, why don't you help us edit a local book on surrogacy? Good?" says Dr. Patel, getting right to the point as usual.

"What?" I'm not quite connecting the dots.

"A colleague of mine is writing a book on surrogacy. We are self-publishing this book to bring about better regulations, and so that we can clear the name of surrogacy in India and around the world. Our writer is Indian. He is very brilliant, but his English is not as good as yours. I know that you too have a passion for helping others to understand about surrogacy. Would you be willing to help us edit this book? You can come to my house for dinner tonight, and we can all work together and get to know one another at the same time. Good?"

"Of course, yes, I'd be delighted to help," I tell her, touched that the iconic Dr. Patel is reaching out to *me* on a personal level for help. I'm very flattered that she wants to get to know me this well, and has invited me into her inner circle. And I can't wait to see what her house looks like! Plus, to be honest, she's right. The babies aren't born yet, and it will be good to have something useful to do while I'm here. I can't be with Vaina 24/7. They follow a strict schedule around here, and the regimen includes a lot of naps. A *lot* of naps. It's one of the reasons I chose this clinic, so I'm not about to break the rules, and I think even if I could spend every waking minute with Vaina, she probably wouldn't be so thrilled with me hovering over her every second of every day. And aside from caring for Vaina, there is literally nothing to do in Anand. Literally. *Nothing.* This is a way that I can help Vaina, and keep myself busy. It feels like fate.

"Good," says Dr. Patel, sealing the deal with a wave of her arm and a swirl of peacock-blue. "My husband, Hitesh, will pick you up at the hotel for dinner. Now, we go and see Vaina." I wonder how long Dr. Patel would have waited to escort me to see Vaina if I'd said no.

Dr. Patel leaves me with Ayisha, the interpreter, who will take me to the surrogate house, adjacent to the clinic. As we walk out of the clinic, we pass ten to twenty women in saris waiting for general medical attention. Though the clinic specializes in fertility services for foreign couples, it also serves the local population with stellar OB/GYN and preventive health services. I smile at many of the women and they smile back. I feel comforted, and I'm surprised at how calm I am. I'm becoming a mother.

At the surrogate house, I walk up the winding tile staircase, at the top of which is a large, mint-green room, with high ceilings and arching windows, thrown open to catch the afternoon breeze. The room is filled with cots lined up next to each other. Healthy, serene-looking young women in various stages of pregnancy are lying about peacefully. Some are drinking tea, others are laughing with one another, still others are quietly studying for the classes they attend while they are here, and some are just resting quietly. The atmosphere is at once lively and tranquil. All eyes and a few giggles are focused on me as I hover hesitantly in the doorway. I am testing the temperature in the room before I enter, and discover that although I feel a little bit like a bright pink Western elephant about to lumber in, I also feel instantly at home. I know in my heart that I'm going to be welcomed here. I've been worried about this. Though I try to remember that we are such different women, in such different places in life, I know that I will be heartbroken if I'm unable to forge a bond with Vaina.

I search the beds for Vaina. I don't see her anywhere . . . was Dr. Patel mistaken? The interpreter points to a bed in the far corner hidden behind a fluttering curtain.

She looks better than I had ever imagined. She is more petite than I remember her, and smaller than she looked in the photo Dr. Patel sent us, but the peaceful smile on her face is just as it was on the first day we met. She is radiant, with a healthy pregnancy glow. Her hair is pulled back into a ponytail. She is lounging in the afternoon sun.

"Hello, Vaina," I say, and she opens her eyes, taking me in and looking as relieved as I feel. I'm touched at how happy she seems to be to see me. My joy at seeing her is indescribable.

"Adrienne," Vaina says, and takes my hand. She doesn't have to say anything else. I can tell from the tears in her eyes exactly how she feels. Then she hugs me. In this moment, we have no need for words. We understand each other completely without them.

I sit down on the bed next to her and she takes my hand and just smiles at me. Then we hug again. Finally I say, "You are looking so well and so pretty, Vaina. I've been thinking about you every day. I had to come. I'm so happy to see you. How are you? Are you feeling well?" The interpreter translates what I have said and I can tell when the interpreter tells her she looks pretty; Vaina smiles shyly and blushes. I also notice that she looks a little tired, and I flash back to the exhaustion I felt when I was pregnant. For a moment, I feel guilty that she is experiencing this instead of me, *for* me.

"I'm well," she says, patting her belly. "You look pretty too. Your babies are getting big."

"Yes," I say, "I can see that. I can't tell you how grateful we are, Vaina, my husband and I, for what you're doing for us. We will be forever grateful."

Vaina hugs me again, and then the interpreter tells us that it is time for Vaina's sonogram. I am going to see my girls!

Vaina holds my hand in the waiting room while we wait for what seems like hours for us to be called. Finally, a nurse emerges and leads us wordlessly into a tiny room with a sonogram on a cart next to what looks like a very cold metal table. I give a sympathetic shiver as Vaina lies down on the metal, and the nurse rubs jelly on her taut, exposed belly.

"Hello, I am Dr. Patel," says a gentle-looking man in a dingy white lab coat, who enters hurriedly and shakes my hand. Patel is as common a name in Anand as Smith is in America, so it should be no surprise that there are other Dr. Patels here. The doctor squeezes Vaina's hand too and smiles warmly. All the anxiety and angst I felt back in San Francisco about lack of communication has ebbed steadily away since I've returned to Anand. No matter who is providing the care, all the physicians, nurses, and lab techs have the most amazing bedside manner: they are kind, compassionate, and responsible.

I take Vaina's hand as the doctor picks up the sensor and begins to run it over her belly, searching for an image to appear out of the the black and fuzzy obscurity on the screen. Vaina is looking at me the whole time, not once at the screen, and I am looking at her. I wonder if we are both avoiding the screen for the same reason: we are both superstitious and don't want to face the picture of possible loss.

"There are the two babies!" I hear the doctor say, and I turn to the screen immediately, squinting to try and make out the images, but it still looks like white blurry blobs. The doctor sees my confusion.

"One baby is looking up here; you see this little girl? And here is the other to the left side," he says, pointing out the details with his finger. Like I said, this is not exactly state-of-the-art imaging technology, but sure enough, I begin to make out the shapes of the babies. Those are *my* two babies. I feel awash in joy and then, just as suddenly, seized by terror. This is right around the time that I lost the baby during my first pregnancy, soon after a bonding experience through a sonogram, much like this one. Now that I have seen my daughters, seen their hearts beat and watched their bodies curl into each other, their existence is very real. I don't think I could bear it if I lost them.

I look back at Vaina, who still isn't looking at the babies on the screen but right at me, as if she's waiting for me to say something.

"Good? Happy?" she asks me, and I look from the screen into her eyes. My terror dissipates. She may fall down, she may get sick, the world may end, but we are in this together, and I have to trust in that. We are safe with Vaina. Everything is going to be okay.

"Yes, Vaina, very happy," I say, and squeeze her hand. She intertwines her fingers with mine and does not let go.

I can't seem to find the right word for this moment. Awesome, inspiring, unimaginable? Yes, it's all this, but even more. Ah, I have the word: *wondrous*. It's wondrous to know that the babies are alive and well inside of Vaina. It's wondrous that I am here, holding her hand as I watch the sonograms of my babies together. And it will be beyond wondrous to be in the room during their birth, sharing the most intimate event that one can share with another human being. Dr. Patel had said that Vaina has approved Alex's and my presence in the room for the delivery, and I am over the moon at the idea that I will be with my girls the second they arrive on this beautiful planet.

My heart is full of something I have not truly felt since Colette died.

I feel *joy*.

❄ ❆ ❄

Vaina holds my hand all the way back to the clinic. I think we're both feeling a little drained. I help her up the stairs and back into her bed at the surrogate house. I can tell that she is ready to sleep. She lies down gratefully as soon as we arrive, sighs, and closes her eyes. One of the surrogates brings us both a cup of tea.

The surrogates here are for the most part, like Vaina, young women from rural villages in the surrounding area. They all have children of their own—this is one of the clinic's rules. Up until now, most of these women have spent their entire lives only within their villages, playing with their children, and spending their time with the other families in their small community. Few have any work, either outside or inside the home, to contribute to the meager household income, and even fewer have more than a few years of schooling. Most are illiterate.

I know that Vaina lives in a very remote village where literally the big event each day is when the shepherds take their goats across the road. Before coming to the clinic, she had never left for more than a day or two. In some ways, her life is simple. She finds great pride and joy in her home, her marriage, and her children. She is a kind, naturally smart woman with a wonderful laugh and strength to her. She is appreciative of all she has, and she maintains this joy by focusing on the here and now. However, she and her husband have had their struggles to make ends meet and to have enough money for food and education for their children. I can't imagine what a courageous leap of faith it was for her to come to this place, away from her home. Despite her assurances to the contrary, I worry that if she were discovered by her neighbors back in her village, she would surely be shunned for doing this. I am glad that she, like us, chose Dr. Patel's clinic, and that thanks to Akanksha, we all found each other.

"Vaina," I say, "I can't tell you how grateful we are for what you're doing for us. I don't know what we would do without you."

"I am happy to bring this joy to your family," Vaina says, her eyes still closed. And then she opens them, sits up, sips her tea gratefully and says in English. "You bring joy to my family too. I'm happy you here."

As soon as I hear her say this, everything suddenly makes sense. Of course I had been feeling anxious and distracted. Of course I felt disconnected in San Francisco. It's because my life was happening thousands of miles away, in this small green room perched above an alleyway in a rural town in India. It's because right now I need Vaina, and she needs me. Vaina is here, my babies are here, my life is here, and finally, so am I.

chapter 9

I am surprised at how easily I've fallen back into the rhythm of life here at Surrogacy Camp. Every day begins with an unpredictable breakfast at the hotel, followed by a walk with a new friend that I meet at the clinic, and a stop at Café Coffee, the one place in town where you can read the newspaper, have a cappuccino, espresso, iced coffee, whatever you like, and it is as good as my favorite Pete's coffee back home. I go every day.

Caroline, my new British friend with the trendy pixie cut, and I are becoming close friends fast. She has a room down the hall from mine. We found ourselves going from smiling across a room to sitting next to each other, to seeking each other out. And of course, there were those strategically timed offerings of saltines, which saved my life on my first day.

Caroline's husband, Cyril, is a very funny guy, which was wonderful to be around during the daily encounters with those enormous needles. But while proximity was the initial driving force behind our friendship, as it is with so many of the people I am meeting here, we are now developing a deeper bond. We have a lot in common. We are the same age, have the same infertility problem, we've both lived in London, we both like coffee, and of course, we are both in India having twins with an Indian surrogate.

In some senses, we Western women who have come to India

to have a baby are all the same. We are all seeking a solution to the same desperate problem. I find myself listening to their stories; there is much in each personal story that I recognize as being part of my own. Everyone here seems willing to share even the most intimate details of their journey. I'm humbled by the pain that everyone here has gone through, and remembering my own experience, I've learned never to judge anyone. Each woman here has traveled a difficult road of her own to get here. I'm not as inclined to share as much of myself with all of the others, but I feel comfortable sharing with Caroline. She and I have similar backstories, and also, of the six other couples who underwent IVF when Caroline and I did, we are the only two couples who were successful. Now, we are both back in India to be part of the pregnancies as they come to term. Those two things alone are pretty rare here.

Each week, five to eight new couples arrive at the hotel to do either IVF or surrogacy. They all have the same shell-shocked looks on their faces that I did when I first arrived (they too must have gotten stuck in a traffic jam dispute between a donkey and a truck on the way from the airport). I also recognize the same heartbreak and steely resolve. Unlike my experience in the States, when I was the pregnancy story that was fearfully whispered about between the nurses, the story that no one wanted to hear, now everyone wants to hear what I have to say. For once in my life, I am the best-case scenario instead of the worst. I am a rousing success story.

These new, eager couples invite me to dinner regularly, and I accept two to three invitations per week. I go, even though I know I will spend the entire night either answering their questions or listening to these couples' stories of heartbreak and their desperate hopes for a successful surrogacy. I am happy to listen, and I help however I can, but there is no quick answer, no magic pill. My story is a successful one, *so far*. And I have seen enough darkness to know how quickly success can turn to despair.

Caroline understands all of this, and it makes our friendship easier. We're both at the same point in the road, understanding all the highs and lows, all that is at stake, so we can cheer each other on when the going gets tough.

Caroline's is not the only familiar face at the clinic from my last visit. Gilde and Arthur, the German couple I had met here on my last trip who had been tied up in a nightmare of red tape trying to get their baby out of the country, were still in a holding pattern, waiting for the coveted exit visa to take their little boy home. I am astounded at their fortitude, and I have to admit I'm a little envious that they were able to just drop everything and spend a year in India. I'm spending just a few months here and the financial and emotional strain is more profound than I had imagined. I still don't completely under-stand why their visa is taking so long. I probably never will and that is why when you do something in India like surrogacy you have to learn how to accept the facts without questions. Surro-gacy in India redefines going with the flow.

Alyssa , our delightful den mother, is also still here. Her son was born a couple of weeks ago, but she is staying on for a bit so the baby can have plenty of time to nurse. Dr. Patel has made sure that another surrogate was available to breast-feed her baby. Formula, potable water, and sterilized bottles can be hard to find in Anand and many of the lactating surrogates are willing to nurse for a fee, which the clinic feels is much better for the babies. Alyssa is, as I remember, using her extensive ex-perience to provide a tireless and valuable resource for the new genetic couples here. She counsels and reassures them con-stantly and never seems to lose patience. She is the go-to person at every confusing bend in the road, of which there are many. She's a terrific guide to the dos and don'ts of Surrogacy Camp. I hope that she is still here for me when it comes time for me to get our exit visas for the girls!

My days are spent shopping the limited stalls in the village trying to find gifts for Vaina. I mostly buy almonds or fruit, sometimes chocolate. There aren't many treats to choose from here in Anand. There aren't any Western clothing shops, or even any bookstores. I did find a shopping mall with lots of battery stalls, which thrilled me just because it was something different. I do get to spend time with Vaina each day in the surrogate house, but this leaves hours to fill in this tiny town. I flip through my Fodor's in vain each day, searching for interesting sights and activities in the area to occupy my time. There is a reason why Anand doesn't make it into any of the tourist books; there isn't much to do no matter how hard you try.

Then I, like many people in Anand, lie down and try to take a nap when the afternoon heat becomes too oppressive. I find it difficult to nap here. Between the traffic blaring, the vendors calling out their wares, people and animals coming and going and never seeming to arrive, and the Muslim call to prayer intoned five times daily from loudspeakers on every minaret atop every mosque as far as the eye can see, it can be difficult to drift off. And then there are the random bursts of fireworks that explode without warning and for no apparent reason. And even with the air-conditioning, there is the heat, which in July is so palpable, so *three-dimensional,* that you can actually hear it. (It sounds like very large mosquitoes.)

These days, though, I find the hubbub comforting; it is an indication of life being lived. Lying here alone in my hotel room, counting the hours until my babies will be born, it's easy to let my mind wander back to the painful landmarks along the road that brought me here. But whenever those memories take me too far out of the moment, the gently woven threads of the Adhan, the Islamic call to prayer, the call to be mindful and to praise God, keep me tied to the present. The loud pronouncements keep me remembering calm.

For these reasons and many more besides, I look forward all day long to my time with Vaina. Most often, we sit together and giggle, eat, hold each other's hands. We are quiet together. Although we don't share a language, we are building up a larger common vocabulary every single day. I no longer miss the verbal communication. We have a much more important dialogue going on between us, with the babies growing in Vaina's womb. It's as if we both understand this, and therefore the silence is rarely uncomfortable or leaden.

I am a classic overachiever. Vaina doesn't look at life as a linear process of ever-ascending self-improvement. There is a fundamental personal and cultural divide between how each of us sees the world and our places within it. Her motivations are less about specific goals and more about just being alive.

I think Vaina wants very much for her children to have a better life than she has, but "better" means something different to each of us. To me, it means a full education, literacy, and travel out of Anand. To Vaina, I suspect it means a more comfortable life in their village. Vaina's village would be considered impoverished by Western standards, but in fact, she is better off than many. She has all the necessities for a sound domestic life—even the luxury of regular electricity—although she has to boil her water before cooking with it or drinking it. This is one of the few dreams she has shared with me: a home with clean running water.

I know that she hopes for a better education for her children, but the truth is, this is impossible unless they leave the village to go to better schools.

Vaina's husband seems to be kind and caring, but it is clear to me that he has an additional agenda—it was a feeling I got based on nothing but my instinct. He then asks us for money in addition to what we are already paying for the surrogacy. I can't help but feel he just looks at me like I am his golden ticket. India, generally, is a patriarchal country where men are in charge of both the public and the private spheres. They are also in control of home finances. Vaina seems to be an obedient and caring wife, one who will do what her husband wants and follow his lead. Their marriage was arranged when they were both teenagers, and Vaina moved straight from her father's house to her husband's. He is the only man she has ever known.

When a woman becomes a surrogate, Dr. Patel opens a bank account for her in her own name. All monies from the surrogacy are deposited there. Dr. Patel counsels each woman on what she could or "should" do with her money. This is more than is offered at other clinics, and I appreciate that Dr. Patel offers these services. After all, she is the director of this clinic and has dozens of patients to attend to. She, personally, doesn't have to take such individualized care with each surrogate. And yet she does. This is another one of the reasons I am so glad I chose Dr. Patel.

I want the surrogacy fee we are paying Vaina to empower her, and to give her a feeling of financial independence that she's never known before. I worry that her husband will spend all the money to buy a new taxi without consulting her, and worst of all, I worry that soon, she will be coerced into doing another surrogacy.

❀๑๑❀๑❀

"Did you enjoy your class today?" I ask her as I bend down and kiss her cheek. Today, I am bringing her a book. It's a story for her children, *Good Night, Gorilla,* by Peggy Rathmann. It's written in English. She prefers when I bring *Vogue* or Danielle Steel.

"Oh, very nice," Vaina says, but doesn't elaborate further. She is engaging in passive resistance. She is very good at this. She doesn't like confrontations, so she tells me enough of what I want to hear—*always*—no matter her own feelings. Thankfully, I'm getting better at reading between the lines.

"I like English class so I can talk to chu," says Vaina, smiling, and grips my hand tighter. I smile and squeeze back.

"What about embroidery? Are you still embroidering your children's clothes in your free time?" Vaina tells me all the time that I ask too many questions. She's probably right. I'm asking too many right now, and I can tell it's making her a little uncomfortable.

"No, well, sometimes," Vaina says, and turns me around so she can oil and braid my hair and change the subject. I think about my own childhood, when my mom would brush my hair into big frizzy curls, and realize that I've come full circle. All the women in the surrogate house, Vaina included, get a kick out of my big hair. They call me "dry curls," and laugh at me. They don't understand why I don't oil my locks into slick shiny plaits like they do. Vaina tries to help me out in that regard, whenever she gets the chance. I guess she too feels a desire to give me what she thinks that I need. One of those things, in Vaina's opinion, is a deep condition.

"If you like," I say, wincing a little as Vaina pulls my braid tighter, "I can help you find a good nursing school after the babies are born. I want to help you and your family however I can."

"So much curls. Pretty Adrienne," says Vaina, smoothing my hair, and then stroking my face. "You look so young for thirty-seven." She always tells me I look her age, which is twenty-six. This is, obviously, a kind exaggeration on her part.

"Thank you," I say, and drop the line of questioning. I realize that aside from being nice, this is also Vaina's polite way of changing the subject.

I think I can see a little envy in the translator's eyes as she interprets what I've said to Vaina. Ayisha is not like Vaina. She has big goals, and somebody like me could help her go a long way toward achieving them. Ayisha would gladly make use of my help and I can tell she is a little resentful that a gift horse like me has been wasted on Vaina.

During these weeks in the surrogate room, I have been learning that while all the surrogates come from humble origins like Vaina, many of the women here are in fact very ambitious. Anya wants to become a nurse in Mumbai. Nadja wants to become a teacher and dreams of one day moving to the United States. And Ayisha, the envious interpreter, wants to go to university to study languages.

Some days, I find myself wishing that Vaina were more like these women, but I'm not sure if it's because I want this for her benefit or mine. If Vaina were more like my own type A hyper-achieving Western linear-thinking self, would she be the calm, patient, nurturing mother for my babies? I feel a very strong need to take care of Vaina, to help her somehow, to do things to make her life better. But what do you give somebody who already has everything that she wants? And how do you inspire someone to reach beyond her current life, when she is perfectly happy with the way things are right now? It's maddening and frustrating, especially when Vaina is helping me in such a profound way. I am longing to return the favor.

It's nap time at the surrogate house, and I can tell that Vaina is tired. She is starting to look *very* pregnant. The more pregnant Vaina gets, the more unpregnant I feel. I am waiting to become a mother, but I don't feel like a mother yet, because I'm not carrying my baby. It's a curious and confusing process. As I watch the women ascend the stairs in a procession of ballooned bellies, and then funnel into the room, each to their own bed, and prepare for sleep I don't know quite how to feel, so I try to just go with the moment, a skill I have only recently acquired. It occurs to me that this too is a gift that Vaina is trying to give to me.

❄※❄※❄

I wander out into the street looking to flag a rickshaw and go back to the hotel for a nap myself. A few steps into my journey I realize that I have unwittingly stumbled upon the annual Rath Yatra celebration, when the deities are carried out into the streets in chariots, borne by thousands of pilgrims, and carried to a nearby temple. The chariot festival is an integral part of the Gujarati culture, so people from all over the region come to Anand to observe it. Many faiths and cultures have contributed to the distinctive melting pot that Gujarat has become, and nowhere is this more apparent than in its magnificent temple architecture. The windows of the temples here are ornamented with carved wooden panels, which capture the intense sunlight and transform it into a cool and subdued tracing of floral and geometric designs. Ornate minarets, balconies, domes, and niches abound, all matchless in the richness and elegance of the artistry that produced them.

In stark contrast to this quiet, sublime elegance, the square surrounding this temple is packed shoulder to shoulder with celebrants all dressed in colorful clothes, carrying fistfuls of incense sticks. I watch, apart and aside as usual, and just breathe in the beauty and energy and pure majesty of this moment. I also realize that I am *never* going to find a cab.

Just a few hours later, Dr. Patel's husband, Hitesh, comes to pick me up for our nightly marathon editing session. Dr. Patel and her compatriots are working on a book designed to "clear the name" of surrogacy and help a world full of Dr. Patel's potential clients to understand that surrogacy is nothing to be ashamed of. I find it moving and very powerful that this tiny enclave of concerned professionals huddle together almost every night in this small village on the Pakistan border, and do what they can to change the world. I'm honored to be asked to be a part of this effort.

Dr. Patel hopes this book will help to establish regulations and restrictions on surrogacy in India to make sure that the rights of the surrogates, as well as those of the genetic parents, are protected. We talk a lot about how the industry has grown so quickly in India, about how surrogacy clinics have sprung up out of nowhere and disreputable operations have taken hold. Dr. Patel told me she accepts only a small percentage of her applicants, but other doctors are not as discerning, and problems have arisen that are giving surrogacy a bad name.

Commercial surrogacy was legalized in India in 2002, and this has given rise to a host of bioethical concerns that Dr. Patel and her colleagues must grapple with every day. To resolve these issues, the country may need to develop a more nurturing system of legal monitoring and regulation.

The obvious appeal for genetic couples of surrogacy in countries like India is largely financial. In America, for example, there is little regulation of surrogacy fees, which can range anywhere from $50,000 to $100,000. We are paying Vaina approximately $15,000, plus any additional cash gifts that we elect to provide.

For the Indian women involved, the salary is very tempting, roughly the equivalent of ten to fifteen years' salary for a man, and so women have come from all parts of the country to register at fertility clinics, to try to become surrogates, and their husbands don't often object. As demand grows, are these women going to be packaged as a commodity, a "womb for rent," as my friend Monica said?

Making a profit from pregnancy is a tricky issue, and is further complicated by questions of globalization and exploitation: is commercial surrogate motherhood oppression or opportunity?

The surrogacy market has grown so large and so quickly that regulations haven't kept up with the pace. So far, fertility clinics do for the most part care well for surrogate mothers, but as the industry grows, there's a concern that the needs of the surrogate mother will be overlooked in order to meet the growing demand. It is this concern that has caused many countries to ban surrogacy altogether. It is a matter of great concern to the people around this table, and they are trying to do what they can to lay the groundwork for a positive surrogacy industry in India, that will benefit mothers the world over. For couples like Alex and me, Indian surrogate mothers are a godsend.

Hitesh is an interesting man, always with a ready wink and a laugh, and never seems to take things too terribly seriously. But you can see when you look into his eyes that he is also a man of enormous depth, which he mostly keeps from everyone but his wife and small group of close personal friends. I imagined that it would take an unusual man to be married to a powerful woman like Nayna Patel in a small town in India, where men usually rule the roost. Instead, far from feeling uncomfortable about his wife's stature, Hitesh seems to enjoy it, and works right alongside her at the clinic without any power struggles. I like this about him. Hitesh was trained as a trauma doctor and works now as the logistical coordinator for all us Westerners. He has a wonderfully calm manner, and always has a joke ready on his lips. He knows that laughter is the best medicine.

"Good evening, Adrienne. How was your day?"

"Fine, thanks. How are you?" I say walking toward the car with him. The Patels drive a new Audi. It's nice, and brand-new, but not too flashy. It's unseemly, in a small town like Anand, to announce one's wealth.

"I have a new joke for you," he says, opening the door for me and then climbing in himself and revving the engine. "What's the difference between an American and a Canadian?"

"What?" I ask, waiting for the inevitable corny punch line that he always produces with a great deal of amusement. No one laughs harder at Hitesh's jokes than Hitesh.

"A Canadian is an unarmed person with health insurance."

"Very funny," I say, laughing along with him as he slaps his knee with one hand, steering his vehicle through the crowded streets with the other.

"I'll bet a Canadian told you that one," I say as he swerves to miss an old man running along the side of the road. How can anyone run in this heat?

"You would be right on that one," Hitesh says, his laughter diminishing as he becomes more serious. "I know your secret, Adrienne," he says then, looking at me and winking.

"What's my secret?" I ask. I'm curious myself.

"You don't come to our house at night for dinner or to work on the book; you come because we have alcohol."

I laugh, even though I think he may have just called me a drunk, in the nicest way possible. He's not wrong. There are no bars in Anand. Gujarat is a completely dry state, but most of the upper-class people have alcohol licenses allowing them to have bars right in their living rooms. I'm not talking about a bottle of scotch and a few lowball glasses. I'm talking about a bar that looks like many places I'd been to in the East Village in New York City. And I'm not going to lie—during those marathon editing sessions, a glass of wine really helps.

Hitesh drops me off in front of the house, and speeds off to parts unknown, probably to have drinks with his friend in another town. Hitesh rarely stays home for dinner during the editing sessions. I think he relishes the opportunity to disconnect for a few hours. Sometimes he reappears to drive me back to my hotel, sometimes he doesn't.

I enter the house and I can tell immediately that despite the lateness of the hour, Dr. Patel has just gotten home from work, because she's still in her sari.

"Hello, Adrienne, so nice to see you," says Dr. Patel, kissing me on the cheek. "I'll be just a few moments. Make yourself at home, everyone will be here soon," she says, and then disappears into her prayer room. Dr. Patel prays to her Hindu gods and goddesses every night. She says she prays for her patients and for her surrogates. She prays for calm pregnancies and healthy babies. I have seen the room only once. It was filled with candles, surrounding an altar piled high with offerings.

I find this side of Dr. Patel so different from the efficient and unemotional woman behind the desk whom I met the first day at the clinic. I have gotten to know Dr. Patel on a personal level now, and I smile when I remember how intimidated I was when I first met her. At our first meeting, I never would have guessed that she prayed for her patients, had a mean backhand at tennis, and had at one time been forced to make a difficult decision between her two great talents, medicine and dance.

The butler hands me a glass of red wine. I'm always the only one who drinks at these gatherings. This doesn't stop me, although it does take some of the fun out of things, so I never have a second glass.

Dr. Patel's home is beautiful. Marble is so cheap here, you can use it for dinner plates, so naturally, there is a grand marble entryway and marble floors throughout the house. The kitchen looks more like a pantry, piled high with huge bags of potatoes, and fruits, and large ceramic canisters filled with beans and rice and spices of every variety.

Dinner here is always vegetarian and always extremely spicy (and always leaves me groping for the Pepto in the middle of the night). Dinner is usually served in the Patels' stunning and tranquil indoor garden, which has minimal furnishings, so you feel like you're dining in a greenhouse. There are windows across the entire back of the house, looking out onto a massive lawn, which is sweeping and open and, in this moment, looks very inviting.

I wander outside and take a seat on the traditional Gujarati swing. The Gujarati swing is the symbol of Gujarati life, and almost every house in Anand has at least one. Swings are installed in courtyards, foyers, balconies, even living rooms. They are like the recliners of Anand, where people spend time knitting, reading, resting, or even praying. I find the swinging very calming, and when I need a break from the group conversation, I often come out here to swing and nibble Dr. Patel's remarkable spicy peanuts. It's very meditative.

Dr. Patel soon emerges in a pair of low-rider Levi's jeans and a T-shirt with the Nike logo, and motions for me to come in. I can see that the circle has gathered, and even at home Dr. Patel is efficient. It's time to go to work.

The editorial circle that Dr. Patel has brought together for the purposes of creating the book on surrogacy is eclectic. The intelligentsia of Anand is an interesting bunch. There is Amrita, a Hindu and a philosophy teacher. She is a wonderful spirit, committed to her work empowering Hindu women, and she has the chutzpah to drive around on a scooter. She has been to the hotel three times to check on me since I met her, which is very kind, and she even gave me a yoga tape to help me relax. Amrita has kind eyes and says that she enjoys living in her small hometown, but there is a sadness about her that makes me wonder if she isn't longing for an expanded horizon. Yet she never travels and says that American music gives her a headache.

Then there is Chetan, a real estate developer who is tall, dark, and handsome, and a real catch by Anand standards. And he knows it. Chetan is the Donald Trump of the area, and owns a lot of land and many local businesses, including the new five-star hotel that's going up downtown. In India, a man is considered "wealthy" if he is fat, and Chetan had lived according to this definition of abundance, but then he became Westernized enough to eschew local tradition and lost most of the weight. The problem is that now, he consumes so few calories that he always seems exhausted and a little out of it. He talks about his diet a *lot*. It seems to simultaneously obsess and exhaust him, and I wonder if he wouldn't be better off sticking with Indian tradition in this instance; what's so wrong with being fat, rich, and happy?

The other philosopher in the group, Sari, is almost like a guru, referencing Gandhi at every opportunity. I can tell that she has struggled with life in Anand. She was born here, but then was sent to London to study. She has recently returned because her family needs her. I can tell that she misses her life in London very much, even more so because she has no idea how she will ever return to it. Her family needs her financial support too much.

Finally, there is the "author" of the book, Ahmed, who is an intelligent young man, if a bit naïve. He tends to take himself far too seriously. He is far from fluent in English, yet he never agrees to any of the changes I want to make. He is forever telling me that the book is "one hundred percent accurate," and that some information needs to be repeated five times in order to be clear. I keep reminding him that I am here as a native English speaker and as someone who is offering a patient perspective, but Ahmed tends to discount my input. Needless to say, this process can be frustrating at times.

Though this book project is a noble undertaking, and my admission ticket into this honorable assembly—my Anand Algonquin roundtable—is a profound honor, writing a book by committee does not necessarily result in the best product. I find our text overly lengthy, pedantic, and cumbersome. Most of our intended readership would be satisfied with a pamphlet rather than the harrowing mini-epic it is becoming over our editorial table. We make slow and halting progress. I read each sentence out loud, opening up each period and preposition for group discussion. It is a classic example of missing the forest for the trees.

"The surrogate mother gives birth and feels nothing for the child. She hands over the baby to the intended family and her life goes on. She never thinks about the family again." I read this and then look at Ahmed. "Do you really think that's true?" I ask. "That doesn't sound right to me. Perhaps we should rewrite this sentence to make it more accurate."

"This statement is one hundred percent accurate," he says predictably. Ahmed believes that he has written a book of mind-bending genius, but to be honest, it's a little hard to take him seriously when he's making statements like this. How could he possibly know what surrogates feel when they give birth? How does he know that they feel nothing? That they never ever think of the baby they bore for another couple? And does he believe that this is what regulators and genetic parents like myself want to believe? Nobody in the group, not even Dr. Patel, objects. I wonder, do *they* agree with this statement? I think about Vaina, and our afternoons together. Will she forget about me once the girls are born? Will her life "go on" without a second of hesitation, without one quick look back? Will I forget about her?

We always work first, then eat dinner. The first night I was there, I ask to use the restroom to freshen up before the meal. You can tell a lot about a culture from its bathrooms, and Dr. Patel's is no exception.

The toilet has four knobs. *Four*. If one is to flush and one is to spray, like a bidet, what on earth can the others do? Since this is not just an exploratory trip to take in the appointments of the restroom this evening, I now face the challenge of figuring out which knob I turn to flush the toilet. I reach toward a knob before my hand snaps back. I really have no other choice, but the idea that I may do something very, very wrong in Dr. Patel's bathroom breaks me out in a cold sweat. I try the knob closest to me and a stream of water squirts all over my dress and onto the floor.

Now that the chance of my returning to the party with my dignity intact is shot, at least I have a one in three chance of picking the right knob next. Knob 2 turns out to be a heater to warm your bum. This is thankfully less messy and seems like quite a good idea. Fifty-fifty shot now. Knob 3, mercifully, flushes the toilet. I do not go anywhere near knob 4.

I mop up the water with a nearby towel, and go back to the dinner table. Everyone is tittering and a few actually break out into full laughter. Apparently everyone has heard knob 1 squirt/ing all over me.

I smile, feeling a slight blush rise in my cheeks, and sit down to dinner. This is my next great dinner party challenge. No forks. Actually, no utensils of any kind. Unlike Ethiopian food, which can be pleasurably eaten with hands due to the yummy heavily moist breads that absorb all the delicious sauce, or even American/Indian food with its *nan*, there is no bread here. Food here is served only with rice. The idea is to mix the *dal*, the curry, and the rice into spicy rice balls that can be eaten with your right hand. You never use your left hand. That is for something else, probably something involved with that fourth knob in the bathroom.

To my uneducated and unsophisticated palate, dinner tastes the same every night. It's always some spicy, sloppy concoction, served with rice, and though I have had much practice, I cannot get down the right hand gestures that will get the food from the plate to my mouth neatly. Gujarat boasts some of the best cui/sine in the world, as I had discovered when I traveled with Jenny to Barola and Ahmedabad. In Anand, everything seems to get turned into a form of Indian grits, and is always a slightly unset/tling shade of yellow. I have a perpetual, obsessive fear that I will get food poisoning while Vaina is giving birth and miss the whole thing. This does not make the food more appealing.

The conversation this evening starts out as usual, comparing Indian and American culture.

"Americans are more superficial than Indians," says Amrita, who has never been to America. "They care about fancy art/work, good wine, gourmet food, famous architects. We don't bother with these things. We care about family, religion, and tradition." I sometimes have to bite my tongue when these blan/ket pronouncements are announced as I have a tendency to re/

semble this portrait. I love good wine and gourmet food, but I am here in Anand because the most important thing is family.

❄❀❄❀❄

It is quite late when Hitesh finally arrives to take me back to the hotel. All I want to do is fall into bed after such a rigorous night editing the uneditable and eating the inedible. Just as I walk into the hotel, Caroline rushes up to me looking very distraught. "Adrienne," she says, "my twins were born tonight."

"But it's too early," I say, and then bite my tongue. Caroline's twins are not due for another few weeks, but I don't need to tell her this. The terror on her wan face says everything. How could this have happened? I wrap her in a tight hug, and Caroline starts to cry.

"They've taken the twins to the NICU," she says between sobs. The NICU is the Neonatal Intensive Care Unit of the hospital in Anand. I have never been there, but it's a word that strikes panic into the hearts of the parents at Surrogacy Camp. When your child winds up at the NICU, something has gone terribly wrong. I feel gripped by a fierce sympathy for Caroline and her babies, and terror for Vaina, who is only a few weeks behind Caroline's surrogate.

As I look in Caroline's eyes, knowing that what I should do is console her and be strong for her, I am overwhelmed by grief and an intense wish that right now, in this moment, I could turn to my *own* mother.

I hold Caroline's hand and tell her not to worry, that everything will work out in the end, even though I'm not sure I believe it. But right now, I need to say it, as if saying it out loud will make it so. I'm not completely sure if I'm trying to convince Caroline or myself.

chapter 10

From the moment that Alex and I began trying to have a family, my mother has been on my mind almost constantly. She was such a dominant force in my life, and left my life much too soon. I wish so much that she were here with me now, watching over my shoulder as Vaina and I brush each other's hair and keep each other company through the long afternoons waiting for my babies to be born. I wish she were sitting beside me at Dr. Patel's editorial circle, discussing my views on the role of surrogacy worldwide, or giggling at the writer who insists that everything he writes is "one hundred percent correct."

I think my mom might be pleasantly surprised at how serious I have become. I don't think she ever quite envisioned me as an ambassador of foreign gestational surrogacy. I was supposed to be the light and fun-loving daughter, who didn't have a care in the world beyond catching the crest of the latest trends and riding them like a wave into shore. I wish so much that she could see me now. I wish so much that she had lived long enough to see the woman I've become, and to meet her grandchildren.

My mom was a vibrant and irrepressible spirit. I believe that I got my sense of adventure and the determination that I needed to make this journey from her. My first memories of my mom are of her brushing my hair. She loved teasing my curls, bringing them to peak volume, and then watering them down so she had to tease them back up once more, just as Vaina does to my hair now.

Just like Vaina, my mom would do this for hours, just spending time with me, silently, lovingly, happily brushing my hair. I would look up at her in those moments, and I remember thinking that she had the most magical blue eyes, and that she was the most glamorous woman in the world. My mom was very beautiful.

My mother and father fell in love at the Philadelphia Art Museum—as my father tells the story of their whirlwind courtship, "it was love at first sight." In order to gain my mother's attention my father would keep going back to the museum to buy more books and get to know her. Their common love for art brought them together and eventually, after a yearlong courtship, they married. They moved to Fort Hood, Texas, where my father was stationed in the military as a doctor. Soon after they had my sister, Allison, then me, five years later.

My father was an ambitious young doctor, and his work eventually brought the family to California, but unfortunately, by then my parents had grown apart. The love that brought them together just couldn't keep them happy, so after twelve years of marriage, sadly, my parents divorced. My mother, however, remained steadfastly rooted in my life, almost more than prior to the divorce.

I was sad when my parents divorced, but it made sense to me, really, even at the time. My mom was in her twenties when she married my dad. She became a wife and then a mom so quickly, and when she was so young. I think she felt, like many women of her generation, that she'd missed out on a lot of things. Those early years of her marriage, staying at home with two small girls, in a strange, new town in Texas were undeniably tough on her. My mom was a spitfire who didn't like being suppressed, so while she did the best she could, in the end she had to seize her life with both hands, and she did. Both my mother and my father seemed to understand that the divorce was for the best, so we understood that too. It was, by and large, a very happy divorce, if there can be such a thing.

My mom and dad had a shared custody arrangement, so my sister and I lived with my dad in Marin County during the week, and spent the weekends with my mom in San Francisco. My mother had become an art appraiser after my parents' divorce, and she took us both to art openings and cultural events every chance she had. It seemed to my sister and me like the best of both worlds. But I suspect that this is also why I learned to be independent, and not lean on one or the other parent too much.

My mom loved five things passionately: me, my sister, art, traveling, and shopping. She had a very sophisticated sensibility: she always wore black, always wore a lipstick color called Orange Flip, and always had a colorful Vera Neumann or Chanel or Neiman Marcus scarf wrapped loosely around her neck. By the end of her life, she had at least a hundred of these scarves.

My mother and I were shopping buddies—an expensive tradition that I carry on to this day, and no doubt will continue with my daughters. My mother and I didn't just enjoy shopping together, we *adored* shopping together. We would shop for anything: clothes, art, home furnishings, even dog apparel—it didn't matter. Every major landmark moment or occasion in my life was made more special because it was a good excuse for my mom and me to go shopping. I remember when I first started looking for a job after college, my mom bought me my first "power black suit," which absolutely refused to wrinkle. My mom told me that as long as I wore that suit, I would never be without work. I found that idea very comforting at a very uncertain time and to this day, I keep that suit in my closet as a good luck charm. Even now, although she is gone, my mom and I are inseparable, joined by all the wonderful memories, and all the beautiful things we found together, on our glorious shopping adventures. Until the day she died, I simply couldn't imagine life without her.

❋⟡❋⟡❋

The day we found out that my mom had breast cancer and that it had spread to twenty-three lymph nodes, I fell to the hospital floor. It was like my legs just went out from under me. My mom peered down on me, lying on the floor, and looked me right in the eye.

"Come on, Adrienne," she said, "let's do something fun!"

After I got over my shock, and literally picked myself up off the floor, I decided to honor my mother's wishes. She had always embraced life—even the tough moments—and she wanted to enjoy what time she had left. And I wanted to enjoy it with her. So we booked a day tour to Gallo Vineyards in Sonoma, had lunch with the winemaker, and walked the property for hours, taking in the rolling green and purple majesty of the North Coast wine country. It was a magical day, and it set the tone for the next two and a half years.

Despite all the bad news we got during my mom's illness, and it was *always* bad news, my mom took it in stride, and focused her energy on planning trips and outings with Allison and me. We carried on with the business of life, but more important, my mom made sure we carried on with the *fun*. She focused on living, and in doing so, she denied death.

But you can't deny it forever. No matter how brave and

noble my mom was, those two and a half years while she was fighting cancer were heartbreaking and exhausting. Allison was my rock during this period. She never let me down. Allison and I would alternate caretaking responsibilities, and just her calm, steadfast companionship was a comfort during those dark days. It's hard to explain how difficult it is to imagine that the woman who brought you onto this planet is not going to be around much longer, but Allison understood everything I was feeling without either of us having to struggle to articulate it.

I hated the thought of not having my mother in my life. She was in so many ways my soul mate. I felt so loved, safe, and totally complete in her arms, in her presence. I would do yoga and go for long walks to try and stay balanced and positive while I was with my mom, but every visit would bring the recognition that she was failing quickly.

I started to dye my mom's hair and give her manicures so she still felt attractive. This in itself was a production. I wanted her to feel as loved, safe, and normal as possible, just like she had always made me feel. It was my way of making her feel loved the way she had made me feel loved when my mom would brush my hair. It was, in some ways, a spiritually gratifying and life-affirming period of my life, but it was also very draining and incredibly dismal.

One night, when the cancer had spread to every part of her body—the lungs, brain, bones—my mother pulled me close to her. She was on hospice care at home, and we both knew that time was short. She could barely breathe, her breath was ragged and forced, and she told me that she wouldn't be around much longer but to always remember how much she loved me. I held her tightly in my arms as she had done for me my entire life.

Her body felt so frail and light; the cancer was eating her from the inside out. My heart was breaking, but I didn't want her to see. I always tried to look healthy and strong around her. It helped us both to deny the obvious.

Finally, I couldn't hold back any longer. I excused myself and went into the bathroom and threw up. I knew that my mom's organs were shutting down, that she was on morphine and hallucinating, and I knew that she would die very soon. There was nothing I could do about it. I felt so helpless, and hopeless. I was beside myself, I couldn't even imagine how I was going to carry on through the next five seconds. Then I remembered what my mom had taught me about how to sur-vive through difficult times, one step at a time. So I just con-centrated on getting through the next moment, and then the next after that. I lived one second at a time, and before I knew it, a full minute had passed. Then another minute passed, and then another after that. Soon, I had managed to make it through five whole minutes. I realized that my mom had given me the tools and the strength I would need to carry on no mat-ter what was happening, and I went back into the bedroom with my mom to face down the inevitable.

We watched *Antiques Roadshow* for hours. I never wanted the shows to end, but of course, they did. Then, when I could see she was getting tired, I kissed my mom good night and told her I would see her in the morning, just like always. The next morning her sister, my aunt Nancy, called to say that my mom had died in her sleep. Aunt Nancy told me that after I had left my mom, she had apparently gotten out of bed, straightened up her office, an act so typical of my mother, then went back to bed, and died.

Alex and I went by her place that early morning to see her one last time before she was cremated. I stared at my mother, stony and still, and she still looked so beautiful. I brushed her hair with my fingertips, kissed her cold, stiff forehead, told her that I loved her, and said good-bye.

❊❦❊❦❊

After my mom died, I cried for a month, and then I dried my eyes, picked up my phone, and dialed my travel agent.

"I want to go someplace fun," I said. "Someplace far away but still in the heart of it all."

"I know exactly what you're looking for," he said. Travel agents in San Francisco are never fazed by metaphorical destination requests like this. "What about India?"

"What about food poisoning?" I said.

"Oh, you'll be fine—as long as you stick to the four-star hotels," he reassured me. A few clicks of his mouse, and my friend Sora Lee and I were booked on a three-week tour.

Ten weeks later, Sora and I were touring the old city of Agra and falling in love with its grandeur and history. We watched the sun set behind the Taj Mahal, listened to the wonderful sounds of people chanting their prayers, and talked endlessly about life and love and loss and what was around the next bend. It was magical, and we never wanted to leave.

The next day we got food poisoning and were praying to go home.

But despite the thirty-six hours of epic dysentery, I had discovered something important. My mom had known what she was talking about. Going fun places really did help. I learned something else too—being in a culture so different from my own is a great tonic in times of distress. Experience is elevated, life becomes larger, and the wounds of the past seem so small in a vast and indescribably sweeping place like India.

My mom taught me many lessons in my life. The postcards

she would send me that always said the same thing, "Your mom loves you," taught me the power of just a few simple words. She taught me to enjoy myself, to be a free spirit, to stand up for myself, to laugh loud and often, and never to spend more than I could afford. My mom taught me that it was important to be a good friend, to eat dessert, not to take yourself too seriously, to be empowered by work, and to know that in the end, you have to be able to rely on yourself. And most important, my mother helped me to understand that when you're climbing a mountain, what's important is to keep moving forward. If you find yourself getting dizzy, just focus on the next ledge, don't look up or down, deny gravity if you have to, just keep climbing.

So it's no surprise that I came back to India, where I had come to heal from the loss of my mom, to face my fears of motherhood—the terror that I might not be able to become a mom, and the terror that maybe I would, and create my own family at last. It is here, in India, that I can hear my mom's voice the loudest, whispering in my ear, reminding me not to falter, reminding me that I am a spitfire just like her, and to never, never, never give up.

chapter 11

My cell phone rings at dawn. It must be one of my clients. I've been conducting business in Anand—my Indian satellite office—but my clients never calculate the time difference correctly. I roll over and fumble for my phone on the nightstand. In the dark, I find it, though I pull a muscle in the process. My bed is the horizontal equivalent of the chairs in the Akanksha clinic. Given half a chance, they'll cripple you for a week. I have to remember to ask housekeeping to flip my mattress. And I have to change my ring tone. The Black Eyed Peas and the morning prayers to Mecca do not make for a dulcet morning duo. I finally get my eyes to focus on the phone. It's not a client. It's Dr. Patel.

My mouth goes suddenly dry and my heart begins to race. "Hello?" I say cautiously.

"Adrienne, you must come to the clinic right away. Vaina is having contractions."

"Wait, what?" I say, turning my head to look at the door, where a young girl has just entered, offering to sell me gum or a watch or antibiotics, I'm not sure which—and my neck starts to spasm. This is another typical scenario in India that reminds me just to go with the chaotic flow. I am getting news about Vania and my almost-born babies as people are barging into my room selling me gum and fake watches!

"Vaina is having contractions. You must come now," Dr. Patel repeats in the slow, even tone that she reserves for problem cases like me, who always ask too many questions at the wrong times and not enough at the right ones.

Once I absorb the enormity of what she's just said to me, I feel like I've had a triple shot of espresso injected directly into my bloodstream. In a country where everyone seems to meander through life, I am constantly accelerating from zero to ninety in the blink of an eye. How does Anand keep sneaking up on me when it moves so slowly?

"But it's five weeks early," I say, quickly doing the math on my fingers and starting to feel a little dizzy. The look on Caroline's face the other night shook me to my core, and I just want my journey to end with a good outcome for both Vaina and my girls. The room starts to spin. My breathing becomes rapid and shallow. This cannot be another tragedy in the eleventh hour. It's just can't be. I won't let it be. But then again, I should know—after cancer, miscarriages, and heartbreak—that I truly have no control over anything. If sheer willpower were enough to sway destiny, I wouldn't be in India right now.

"Is everything okay?" I manage to croak.

"We'll do a sonogram this morning. Come to the clinic please. Not to worry. Many twins are born early." And then she hangs up. Sometimes I wish Dr. Patel weren't a woman of so few words.

I throw on the nearest pair of pants and a T-shirt and charge out the door. Wait. I should bring something for Vaina. I bring her something every day and today is definitely not the day I want to show up empty-handed. I can't take time to go by the big bazaar, so I turn back to my room and grab the stack of magazines by my bed, shove them in my bag, and hurl myself downstairs into the early-morning chaos to hail a ride. I'll take anything this morning: rickshaw, moped, car, or cow, I don't care. I just want to get there to be with Vaina and my girls. I can't believe this is happening now. I really can't believe it. I start to feel something alongside the panic, something a little like . . . is that excitement? I think it is. Maybe this isn't tragedy in the wings. Maybe it's joy. I could be a mother starting today. If only I could find a damn rickshaw!

Finally, a rickshaw pulls over, and I climb in. We make incremental progress, since it's the morning rush hour. I wish this driver had Abhi's miraculous ability to part the traffic seas. Should I call Alex? I want to hear his voice, but frankly, I don't even know what's going on myself, so what can I tell him? All I would do, most likely, is upset him, and I know he'll have a million questions.

We come to a rattling halt outside the clinic. The entrance, as usual, looks as if nobody has moved a centimeter from where they were the last time I arrived. In this moment, trapped between sheer terror and exhilaration, I find this reassuring. As much as my life may change in the next few hours, it's nice to know that I can count on some things to stay the same. Perhaps this is part of Vaina's positive outlook and the cultural emphasis on doing things slowly, but with meaning. The Zen of sitting still begins to dawn on me.

The receptionist with the movie star smile beams at me like she does every day, but this time she actually says "Hi, Adren." I find this comforting as well. The staff knows me by name, or at least a version of my name. I've become something of a celebrity around the clinic. I can tell that even the new patients in the waiting room recognize me. Dr. Patel tells at least six people a day that my twins are due anytime now, maybe even today. I'm one of her success stories, or at least, I *was*.

"Dr. Patel is with a patient now, but she'll see you very

shortly," a nurse says to me, motioning me toward the waiting area. I swear the picture of Oprah winks at me. I take a look at the waiting room, where a young couple from Australia sits anxiously awaiting their first appointment with their surrogate. They look so clean and expectant, as nervous as a new bride and groom before their first dance. I feel like I've traveled a million miles since the day I was the expectant mom, sitting in those chairs waiting to meet Vaina for the very first time. "I'll be across the way," I tell the nurse, who nods her head in agreement, although I don't think she's understood me. In India, when you are in doubt, you just agree with whoever is speaking to you, so this is not reassuring, but the clinic is too small for them to lose me for long, and besides, this is Dr. Patel's kingdom. If she needs me, she will have me found.

I walk up two flights of stairs at the clinic to the third floor, where they house the surrogates who are close to giving birth—this is the transition area where they spend their last four to six weeks of the pregnancy, so they are close to Dr. Patel and any medical services they might need in an emergency. I don't know where Vaina is; she could be the patient Dr. Patel is seeing right now or, since the contractions were just starting, she could be resting in her room until it is time. I should have asked the nurse this question. *Alex* would have asked that question, rather than wandering aimlessly through the corridors. After all the effort and planning that have gone into this day, how have I forgotten to ask the most critical and basic: *Where is Vaina?*

I walk into one of the surrogates' bedrooms, with its enveloping green walls and fluttering muslin curtains. The light from the television flickers innocuously in the corner. There's an Indian soap opera on this morning. The women are riveted. I look around and spot Vaina resting peacefully on her bed. She looks absolutely fine, and I exhale for the first time since I answered the phone this morning.

Vaina's husband is curled up on the floor beside her bed, holding her hand. For many Westerners, arranged marriages are so foreign, so far removed from our notions of romantic love and lifetime commitment, that it is hard to imagine that anything more than mutual respect or friendship could develop for a couple like Vaina and her husband. As much as I have grown to care for Vaina over the past few months together, I have had a harder time getting a read on her husband. He always seems sweet, but without his wife to cook his food, wash his clothes, do his mending, and watch his children, he is lost. I can't help but wonder if their relationship is based more on the convenience of having someone else to share the household responsibilities with than a true connection to each other. And yet, this moment proves that their relationship is based on more than commitment, shared values, respect, and appreciation. I see now that she is his rock, and he is hers. They have what Alex and I have, what every married couple should have: love.

I am hesitant to intrude on their moment together, but I also want to be involved. I approach them and ask, "Vaina, are you feeling okay? Do you need anything?" She opens her eyes and smiles. When Vaina smiles, her whole face glows with youth and pleasure, and she looks like a fourteen-year-old girl rather than the experienced twenty-six-year-old Indian wife and mother she actually is. I realize that I am really coming to love her, but it's hard to say quite how.

"Hi, Hadrin. Miss you," Vaina says and closes her eyes again. I sit down on the bed beside her and take her other hand. Her husband gets up from the floor and nods to me politely, then goes out into the courtyard for a cigarette. I can see him glancing up nervously at our window every few seconds through the clouds of smoke hanging in the humidity like fog. I can see even through the thick mist how worried he is about his wife.

"Do you want anything to eat? I brought some almonds," I say, shuffling around in my bag.

"No, good," Vaina says. *Of course she isn't hungry, you idiot.* She's having contractions. Nobody wants to eat when they're having labor pains. Oh, my God, Vaina is in *labor.* Is this going to happen *today*? Am I going to become a mom today? After all the waiting, it all feels like it is moving too quickly and I can't quite catch my breath.

"You look pretty. Pretty eyes. Pretty. So different," Vaina says sleepily. Then she takes my hand and places it on her belly. I feel a little kick.

"Don't worry, Hadrin," she says, and squeezes my hand.

Vaina is in labor and she is worrying about me. I suddenly feel pangs of guilt; this lovely woman, whom I didn't even know a year ago, is going through all this for Alex and me. She moved out of her home, spent nearly eight months away from her friends and family, only seeing her own children sporadically, all for a couple she didn't really know. All to bring into the world two little girls whom she will never really know.

It is only in this moment that the full weight of what we have asked of Vaina, and what she has agreed to do for us, hits me. It should be me going through these contractions. It should be me facing the risks of premature labor. It should be the inside of my belly those babies are kicking. This last makes me think of the kicks that I felt during my first pregnancy with Colette. As much as I feel guilt for what I have asked of Vaina, I also am envious. She is having an experience of my children that I will never understand myself, and even though my head understands why this is so, my heart still wishes that I could have carried all my children to term.

It's almost indescribably odd, this experience of having a baby without being pregnant or giving birth. The situation has everything to do with me—it is entirely of my design—yet nothing in this moment has to do with me at all. So I do whatever I can to insert myself into the conversation, even if only to distract her from her labor pains.

"What is your favorite color?" I ask Vaina, trying to engage her in a little idle chitchat. Ayisha translates what I've said, and when Vaina understands the question, she blushes. Is it possible to have an embarrassing favorite color?

"Red," Vaina says, and then she blushes even brighter. Then I understand. Vaina makes bold choices in a country that insists on understatement, particularly where women are concerned. Even after all these weeks together, there is so much about her that I don't know.

"Hello," says Dr. Patel, who I didn't realize had come to stand behind me. I can see Vaina's husband hovering in the doorway, trying to get a glimpse of his wife, but he doesn't come closer. Everybody keeps a safe distance when Dr. Patel is doing her rounds, and Vaina's husband is no exception. Everyone in Dr. Patel's world, including me, has been carefully trained to know their role. If we weren't, this clinic could never manage the work. Everything has to run like a well-oiled machine, or chaos ensues, even if this means that a concerned husband must stay off to the side while his wife meets with her doctor.

"How are you feeling?" Dr. Patel asks Vaina in English. I'm grateful to be able to follow along. Vaina nods and smiles, but then winces as a new contraction begins to roll in. I can see that Vaina is worried. She takes pride in what she's doing for us, and I know that she doesn't want to disappoint me. Again, admiration, gratitude, guilt, and terror wash over me like a wave. Dr. Patel briefly listens to the babies' heartbeats, takes Vaina's pulse, and briefly examines her. Satisfied, she squeezes first Vaina's hand, then mine.

"I checked the sonogram, the babies are fine. These are just false labor pains." I feel instant relief, with just a dash of disappointment. Sure, I had thought that I wasn't ready, but I also thought that I might become a mother today.

"I'd like the babies to cook a little longer, so I won't pull the stitch that we put in your cervix. From now on, strict bed rest," says Dr. Patel, and looks at both of us to make certain that we've understood and points her finger for emphasis. Why is she looking at me? I haven't been taking Vaina out clubbing. Then it dawns on me: I'm the entertainment.

"I brought some magazines," I say, remembering the rags I'd somehow thought to cram into my bag on my mad dash out this morning. Dr. Patel smiles at me the way she does when I'm on the right track.

"Do you want to look at them?" I ask Vaina, dying to be somehow useful in this process.

"Okay," says Vaina, without mustering much enthusiasm. False or no, these are labor pains she's experiencing. I'm not sure I'd be feeling like paging through *Vogue* and *New York* magazine either.

"Very American," I say, conceding the obvious. Sitting here, in this humble room, flipping through the pages with my Indian surrogate, these familiar images of fashion models are starkly out of place. It's culture shock, plain and simple. I wonder, do I stick out in the room like these pictures do? I can tell that these postcards from the world I inhabit look a little silly to Vaina, and even a little scandalous, but she doesn't say anything.

She doesn't want to hurt my feelings. But does she think that I'm a little silly too?

Vaina furrows her brow and closes her eyes. She's having another contraction. When it passes, she opens her eyes again and smiles, but I can see that she's tired, and feeling as pregnant as I feel unpregnant. Now that we adjusted to our scare this morning, we're both more than ready for these babies to be born.

"I'll let you rest, but I'll be back tomorrow," I say, deciding to stop trying to make conversation. What's happening right now is beyond language. It is beyond our control.

❀✿❀✿❀

Before heading for home, I decide to visit Caroline and Cyril's babies at the NICU hospital, which is down a dirt path about one block away from the clinic. From the moment I enter the hospital, it's absolute chaos. Like the clinic, the NICU hospital is a bit dismal. The babies were delivered at the clinic but their lungs had not fully developed and there were some respiratory issues, so they were moved to the NICU section of the hospital. The walls of the hospital are covered with peeling, chipped paint, and of course air-conditioning is completely nonexistent. The lights flicker. I hope that this is because the bulbs are burning out and not because the electricity supply is unreliable.

Coming from San Francisco, I am accustomed to hospitals that are calm, clean, and orderly. Here in Anand, I believe that the medical care is very good. I have met the most professional and capable doctors here, like Dr. Patel, doctors whose knowledge and wisdom in the face of such confusion is nothing short of miraculous—but the "frills" of new paint and air-conditioning would go a long way to support that belief. I sit down in the waiting room, which is reserved especially for Western visitors, and is air-conditioned. It offends my morals—I believe in air-conditioning for all—but I am not so principled as to sit in the hot air in protest. I don't see Caroline or Cyril. They must have gone out for a bite to eat. They had been at the NICU almost 24/7 since their twins were born.

Finally, a nurse comes and leads me to Caroline's babies. They are so tiny in their incubators. Both babies look identical to me, even though they are a boy and girl. They are so small I can't tell if they resemble either of their parents. They look sick and very pale, and that breaks my heart. One of the babies is having so much trouble breathing it is difficult even to look at him or her. I send them positive thoughts and prayers, and reassure them that they will be fine. That is really all anybody can ever do. It just feels like so little.

I have been so grateful for Caroline's friendship here. We can talk about being excited, about being impatient, and about what it feels like to be in India for one of the most important experiences of our lives. We have gone through most of the legs of this journey together, walking this road in lockstep, until today. Now Caroline has gone ahead of me, and the road has led to the NICU. I hope that it doesn't end here.

On the way home I stop off at the big bazaar to try to find a gift for Vaina. Now that she is on bed rest, I am going to have to get very creative to keep her entertained until the babies are ready to be born. With the birth so near, I realize that this phase of our friendship or courtship or business arrangement, or whatever I've decided to call it this week, is going to end soon. I've heard from Alyssa and other mothers here that as soon as the baby is born, you and your surrogate begin the separation process. This is as it should be. It is as it has to be.

The clinic supports this separation process in postcare, which is why your surrogate generally isn't the one to breast-feed the baby; another surrogate who is lactating is put in place to breast-feed the baby. Although some couples opt to use formula from the beginning, the clinic offers breast-feeding as an option because even a few weeks of breast-feeding give the babies a better start nutritionally and provide important immunity protection to the baby that you can't get with bottled formula. Plus, good formula is hard to come by in Anand, as are reliable sterilization techniques.

For obvious reasons, the fear is that if the actual surrogate breast-feeds the baby she carried to term, a bond will start to develop and the separation would be more dramatic, so there are not only other surrogates available to perform this necessary function, but the clinic has breast milk banks that parents can buy from to feed to their own babies by bottle, which makes the process even more removed from the surrogate mother experience. I want the connection between Vaina and me to be strong and enduring. I wish that it were easier for us to talk. I wish we had more in common. I wish I could offer her more; at times our relationship feels very one-sided. We are from such completely different worlds, but then again, this is part of the reason why our bond is so special.

I can tell that Vaina is ready to get back to her life, and I have to say, I don't blame her. I long to go back to my regular life as well: walks in the park with friends, business calls that happen during regular daylight hours, cappuccino, television, snuggling on the couch with my husband. I miss Alex so much, it physically hurts, and even though Vaina sees her husband and children regularly, it is not enough.

Obviously, Vaina and I have one very important thing in common that holds us together right now. We both want the same thing, the successful birth of two healthy baby girls, but I am greedy. I want more, I want a connection that will bind us together through the birth and beyond. I have no idea what this bond might look like once the girls are here, but after she has played such an important role in my life and the lives of my children, I can't imagine never seeing this woman again.

The thought of losing Vaina frightens me. At this moment, I hear my mother talking to me, telling me to start counting sheep because it would relax me. Just focus on the sheep, Adrienne, she tells me, and keep counting, and your mind will go to a more calm place. So this is what I do.

I walk past an appliance store that's giving away a free micro-wave oven. The latest impeccably turned out Bollywood leading lady is announcing the winner from the back of a truck, before a crowd of what looks like literally thousands of people, all standing in breathless anticipation to see who the lucky winner will be. I hope whoever wins has electricity.

Next to the appliance store, I notice a stall that is put to-gether with muslin, plywood, duct tape, and chewing gum. In the corner of the stall is a somewhat battered-looking drum and a cymbal surrounded by a few sad-looking dolls. Music and rhythm are languages that everybody understands. I im-pulsively buy the drum on the spot without even trying it out—a tiny plastic drum with two plastic sticks and a cymbal. I feel so excited to share the drum with Vaina and have some fun with her. I'm so sure that I want this that I don't even hag-gle, which is unheard of.

I'm thrilled with my purchase until I realize this stall prob-ably does not deliver. I have quite a time trying to navigate my way back to the hotel. Rickshaws pass me by pretending not to notice me, and mopeds are out of the question. Finally, a rick-shaw takes pity on the crazy American lady standing on the corner with a snare drum and a cymbal in her hands and pulls over. The driver very kindly helps me load my latest brain storm into the back of the cab, and drives me to the hotel.

I make quite a scene as I enter the lobby of the Laksh Hotel. I stop all six discussions about eggs and fertility dead in their tracks as I rata-tat-tat through the doors. Alyssa looks up at me and grins and helps me unload my cargo. Alyssa is always right there with a hand when I really need one. Alyssa just seems like an expert. She is constantly reading books about fertility and this is her third time in India for fertility issues.

"Everything all right?" Alyssa asks. Her eyes search mine, and I know that she must see the wear and tear in my face. It's been quite a day.

"Yes, fine, thank God. We thought that Vaina was going into labor early, but it turned out to be premature labor pains. She's on bed rest. Dr. Patel has put me in charge of the entertainment committee, hence the drums," I say, smiling sheepishly.

"That ought to shake things up at the surrogate house," Alyssa says, laughing.

"Well, I'm trying to find ways to communicate with my surrogate without language," I explain. "It's hard to feel a connection when our translator is always cutting in."

"That's natural," says Alyssa. "Don't worry, everything will unfold just as it's supposed to. Remember, no matter how distant and removed you may feel from this process at times, there are two very precious gifts that will connect you to her in a deeper and more profound way than English or Gujurati could ever articulate." She pats my back and points toward the lounge. "There are some new couples here today who would love to hear your story. Come and sit down with us and let them look at you. They could all use a little inspiration. You remember what it's like." It's true, I do. I look over toward the couches and see anxious, eager faces. Right now, they think that they have lived through the hardest part of this journey. They have dealt with the ugliness of infertility: the envy they feel when they see complete strangers pushing a stroller, the distress at not conceiving month after month after month; or perhaps, like me, they know the wonder of pregnancy followed by the heartbreaking agony of loss. They have lived through this, and now, they laugh at the troubles they find here—the mosquito bites, the rusty air-conditioner—because nothing compares to what they have been through. The truly hard days are behind them.

That's what Alyssa wants me to tell them, but I know that it is not so simple. Now, rather than cry myself to sleep thinking about the babies I lost, I lie awake thinking about the babies I am too afraid to hope could really be mine. I had thought it would be the grief that would be my undoing, but I was wrong. It's the uncertainty.

It's impossible to say no to Alyssa, so we ask Fatima to put the drum in the luggage room, and I go and sit down in the dining room to meet the new campers.

It is truly wonderful to meet couples from all over the world who are on the same journey as I am. There are only a few familiar faces from when I first came here for my IVF treatments several months ago: Alyssa, Caroline and Cyril, Gilde and Arthur. The guests here go through a total sea change every couple of weeks, and it's impossible to keep track of who is here for what. It begins to feel like an ever-changing gallery of hopeful and slightly dazed faces, eager to be embarking on a new road. Few stay long enough to become friends.

I am unusual. Most couples are here only for the two weeks it takes to go through IVF and for two weeks just after the birth to do all the necessary paperwork. Between conception and delivery, they return home to their regular lives. I think many of the biological mothers choose to return home because this experience is so unfamiliar and frightening. Many believe that their role as the genetic parent is to pay the surrogate, bring a gift, and then leave her alone, patiently waiting for the birth. In some ways, that is easier; it's certainly a less emotionally and psychologically complicated route, and even Dr. Patel encourages it.

Some women don't even come to the clinic for IVF. Instead, they send their cryogenically frozen fertilized eggs here for implantation and then arrive to pick up the baby after delivery. I can't begin to imagine this. Having a baby shouldn't be like Internet shopping. For me, it was very important to be part of the whole experience at every stage. Every phase of the pregnancy was important, from start to finish, and there is so much that I won't experience, so at the very least, I wanted to be present.

I sit down with Alyssa and am of course immediately bombarded by questions, and I ask some of my own. I know the answers to most of the questions I ask but all I want is to bond with her as everything else feels so foreign to me that I feel calm asking her familiar questions and getting familiar answers. They all ask me pretty much the same things: things that they don't tell you about in the brochures, things that only someone going through the process can fill you in on. How is my relationship with my surrogate, and how friendly should they be with *their* surrogates are common questions. There is some thoughtful, well-written literature out there on the subject of surrogacy, but nobody really talks about this central relationship between the biological and the surrogate mom, not even Dr. Patel. So I try to describe what my experience has been with Vaina thus far, but I certainly don't have all the answers, I'm figuring things out as I go along, myself.

In the book I've been working on with Dr. Patel's group,

the surrogate has no feelings for the baby after the birth. I'm sure each and every surrogate feels differently about the child she carries, and it is certainly a relationship that has many layers. All I know is that for me, it has been critical and life-changing to be part of the pregnancy with Vaina. It is a complex bond, and a powerful one, whether we are together or thousands of miles apart, whether it lasts forever, or for just a season.

Even though Vaina and I don't share a language, we have creatively found ways to communicate. I draw pictures, show her photos from magazine articles, and do charades. I've learned that she says so much with a wink, a shrug, a hand gesture, or a sly smile. We have started to get to know each other by discovering other forms of communication. Like a drum set.

In the dining room, I wind up in a conversation with a furniture importer who has spent $200,000 on ten unsuccessful IVF attempts and is still trying. I realize when I speak to women like this that I've been very lucky. They realize it too, and it's almost as if they feel that when they're around me, my luck will somehow rub off. Sometimes it makes me feel a little uncomfortable, especially now, when I'm petrified that my luck will run out. It's not that I'm expecting the worst, or feeling superstitious in any way. But it's happened to me before, more than once.

I've never been a particularly religious person, but in India I find myself praying. So much is out of my hands in this country, and I'm learning that I have to give up control and focus on faith. Whether you believe in God, or the benevolence of the universe, it's important to have something to turn toward. Prayer and yoga have become as important as eating and breathing for me. They make me feel more at peace. So, in addition to answering their questions, I tell the couples coming up behind me to be strong but to understand that it's okay to be emotional, to remember that this stage of becoming a parent is part of the longer journey, and to be patient. I was lucky and my IVF treatment was successful the first time; for others, multiple IVF cycles are necessary. As Vaina is teaching me, it is important to focus on and appreciate the here and now, even when everything in you wants to stretch into the future. It's hard, but you have to hold on to what you have now, and let that be enough. It's the mantra I've been repeating to myself over and over again, since this all began. By now, I almost believe it. Almost.

❋ ❦ ❋ ❦ ❋

When I finally make it back to my room, I take a deep breath and call Alex. I can't believe I convinced myself that I could go through these months without him. After today, I feel alone, scared, and a little angry that he isn't here with me. With two little ones on the way, however, we will soon be a family of four, and we need Alex to keep working and earning income up until the very last moment. I've done my best to continue working from Anand, but it hasn't been easy, and we are feeling the financial strain. We'd both agreed to this plan, but just because I know in my head that he should be in San Francisco, in my heart, I want him by my side.

"Hi, Alex," I say, trying to sound upbeat.

"Hi, my love. How's it going over there?" he asks, and as soon as I hear his voice, I instantly feel at home.

"Okay, I guess. We had a little excitement today because Vaina started having contractions," I say, trying to keep my voice as stable and routine-sounding as possible. I'm channeling Dr. Patel. "It's fine now, it was false labor, but it gave us all quite a scare."

"I can imagine," says Alex, the relief plain in his voice. "Thank God everything is okay now. Everything *is* okay now, right?"

"Yes," I say, wishing more than ever that he were here. I want to bury my head in his chest and feel his arms around me. "I miss you."

"I miss you too," he says, and I can tell he feels the distance too. "I think I should come over there right now. I don't want you going through this on your own," Alex says. We've been together so long, I know that he can hear the fear and anxiety in my voice even when I am putting on a brave front. I've never been the kind of girl who looks for a white knight to rescue her. I've always been more than comfortable relying on myself, but that is one of the joys of marriage, and it's a lesson I know I need to learn before we become parents. I don't have to do it all by myself anymore, and with twins on the way, I can't.

Alex is waiting for my answer, and I realize, it's always been up to me. If I'd asked him even once he would have been here with me. And he would be here tomorrow if I asked him now. I think about Vaina and her husband, the way he held her hand. Do I need Alex to travel halfway around the world to come hold mine?

"That's okay," I say, realizing as I say the words that it really is. "I don't want you to cause problems for yourself at work for no reason. I'm fine here on my own for a few more weeks. It won't be much longer now!"

"How long, do you think?" Alex asks, and the excitement I hear in his voice sparks my enthusiasm. Talking to him always reminds me that this is a joyful event, not a dreadful one.

"Two weeks, maybe three. I'll call you just as soon as I know anything so you can be here holding my hand when the twins are born."

When the twins are born. When *our* twins are born. Our twins are going to be born! I take this in and become breathless again. Because of all our false starts, I think that I never truly allowed myself to revel in the moment. Until those babies are delivered, I will continually have to remind myself, *Adrienne, this is* really *happening.* And then I get excited all over again, giddy with possibility, until my obsessive fears that something somewhere will go wrong in the last minute return. It's an exhausting, cruel cycle.

chapter 12

These babies are stubborn. They don't want to come out. I am
pleased about this because I want them to be as healthy and
heavy as possible—I want them, as Dr. Patel says, to "cook" a
bit longer—but that doesn't mean I'm not impatient. Vaina is
still on bed rest. If all goes well, she will deliver Wednesday or
Thursday of next week. One of the babies is only three and a
half pounds, which is small, and she is also in breech position.
The other is head down and weighs around four pounds, which
is perfect. With one of the babies being breech, Dr. Patel may
have to do a C-section, but I'm hoping that the baby will turn
before delivery. Vaina seems to be comfortable and content,
but she is having contractions daily, so who knows! I'm getting
nervous, but I do have so much confidence in the doctors and
nurses here.

These last days before the birth seem outrageously long. I
still go to the market daily to buy Vaina a gift, then off to the
surrogate house to spend a few hours with her, and then the rest
of the day is mine to fritter away as I wish. I have now been invited to a few different outings with other genetic parents—to
the theater, book readings, dinner parties—and every few nights,
I go to Dr. Patel's to continue editing the never-ending book on
surrogacy. The process is beginning to exhaust me, but I enjoy

the company of the writers and philosophers who are a part of Dr. Patel's salon.

Most nights the conversation in the group inevitably turns to all things Gujarat, the land of Mahatma Gandhi, inhabited by peace-loving and enterprising people. They tell me that the most educated people in India come from Gujarat, and that Gujaratis are credited the world over for their business acumen. I learn that in days gone by, Ahmedabad was acclaimed as the Manchester of India.

We talk a lot about Gujarati literature and discuss at length the ways in which Indians write differently from Americans. They seem to be a little dismissive of American authors. They seem to really gravitate toward spiritual and self-help books, anything that has to do with God and being calm. Occasionally, I take the opportunity to make a couple of jokes about how the Indian writers, like Ahmed, like to repeat themselves to really get the message across. That goes over like a lead balloon.

I seem to be the most interested in yoga of this literary crowd. Amrita, one of the writers, brought me a yoga tape last week and explained to me that most people in India do yoga at people's houses, in private, or spiritual leaders may hold small classes, but it is generally less commercial and more private. Yoga in India is less about Lululemon and yoga mats and tight buns, and much more about breath.

The Patels' daughter is getting married next month, and Dr. Patel glows with excitement whenever she discusses plans for the wedding. She is going to perform a duet of classical Indian dance with her daughter at the ceremony, and they've been rehearsing for months.

Indian weddings are very colorful events, filled with ritual and celebration, that continue for several days. Wedding traditions vary across religion, caste, ethnicity, language, region, and so on, but traditionally, all Indian weddings are structured into pre-wedding ceremonies and wedding day ceremonies. And Indian weddings are enormous affairs, often with four hundred to a thousand people attending, many of whom aren't even known to the bride and groom.

Though most Indian marriages are arranged, some couples in urban areas marry for love. The true Indian wedding is about two families joining socially; there is much less emphasis on the individual. Dr. Patel's daughter, a doctor herself, is marrying another doctor, and she is marrying for love. Dr. Patel says that they are very happy. Her only sadness is that her daughter has chosen to live outside Anand, and outside her mom's powerful influence in this area.

Aside from my nights at Dr. Patel's, I live for the mornings I spend with Vaina. She has been tired most days, so I've been waiting for the perfect moment to spring the drum set on her. This morning she is feeling more energetic, so I decide today is the day.

The atmosphere has been a little heavy in the surrogate house; just waiting for birth and counting contractions keeps us constantly on edge. I want to lighten things up a little, and spend a few moments as we were before everything began, just laughing together.

I rattled and crashed my way into Abhi's car this morning and he helped me set up the drum and cymbal in the common room. Now I am perched in front of my battered drum, making a spectacle out of myself as I attempt to teach the surrogates how to do a solo just like the garage bands back in San Francisco. I've never taken a drum lesson in my life, but for one afternoon I think I'm channeling Tommy Lee and Keith Moon.

I feel a little out of my element, as usual, but I have to say, the experiment with the international language of syncopation is going off with a bang. Everybody looks very amused, though it's less about the drum than about how preposterous I look playing it. The legs of the snare drum are wobbly, and it tips over every time I try to get fancy and show them my drumroll. It's so good to see all these women smiling and laughing together, and it's a relief to experience something together without translation.

I offer the drumsticks to Vaina, who at first shakes her head no. She's less familiar with making a spectacle of herself than I am. But her friends urge her on—the art of peer pressure is, apparently, universal—and finally, she takes the sticks and sits down in front of the drum. She looks up at me, blushing with embarrassment, but with a wicked glint in her eye.

"What do I do?" Vaina asks me, staring at the sticks in her hands.

"Bang the drum," I say, motioning with my hands. She looks a bit horrified. She doesn't like attention. She's a quiet person, not accustomed to making noise. But I know that there is that wild streak, the part of Vaina that likes the color red, and again I see the flicker in her eyes as she raises the sticks and gives the drum a couple of good hard rata-tat-tats. Then she looks triumphant for a brief moment, before the embarrassment sets back in.

It's an eye-opener sitting with the women in this room every day. No chitchat or exchanging of cultural values and perspectives. Mostly, they sit and stare as I spend time with Vaina, and I can tell they're trying to figure out what to make of me. None of the other genetic moms comes to this house as often as I do; everyone here knows my name. I represent something that simultaneously attracts and repels them—a future they're not sure they want to embrace.

Women in India, or at least the women in this room, are in transition. Just like India itself, they seem trapped in that ambiguous nether realm between then and now. Indian girls in particular are expected to be quiet, obedient, and dutiful. Women marry young—I would have been an old hag by Indian standards when I married Alex at thirty-two—and are supposed to submit to their husbands. Like Vaina, many move straight from their fathers' homes to their husbands', never experiencing the independence that many Western women are able to enjoy. Defying your parents is still a very edgy concept, but even in a small place like Anand, where few women work outside the home, it is no longer unthinkable, and the younger generation especially is beginning to think beyond its own backyard.

The surrogates vary widely in terms of how they feel about their surrogacy experience, and what they want to do with their money and with their lives once this exercise is complete. Caroline's surrogate, Frida, is going to put some of the money toward her children's education and some into the school in her village where she is a teacher. Ayisha, the translator, was a nurse's aide at the clinic before she became a surrogate. Her sister was also a surrogate in the house with her. After her surrogacy, Ayisha became a translator, thanks to the language classes she took while living in the surrogate house. Being a translator pays better than being a nurse! She is very good at her job as a translator, but I get the sense, just a feeling I have, that she and her sister are desperate for money in a way that the other women are not.

One surrogate, whom the other women call the Gujarati equivalent of Mama, is a little older, and has a sweet and maternal air about her. She told me that being a mother was the love in her life. She seems to be more concerned with helping families have a child, rather than with how a surrogacy fee will change her own life. She always asks me if I like India in a way that suggests that if I don't, I ought to reconsider my position.

Some of the women are planning to start small businesses in their village when they return home; others intend to give the money to their husbands and never question how they choose to spend it. I suspect Vaina is in this second category. Others think they will do a little of each, and try to keep a foot in both worlds; at the very least, many intend to put some money away for their children's education.

Vaina seems content with her traditional lifestyle. Yet Vaina, like all of these women and lots more just like them, is taking on a role that has heretofore been virtually impossible—the main breadwinner in her family. This is Vaina's second surrogacy—surrogates at Akanksha are permitted to do the service up to three times—but because the first surrogacy attempt was unsuccessful, she will be able to do this twice more after giving birth to my babies. She's told me that she will sign up again to help her family. I can tell she feels empowered by the ability to make such a large amount of money for her family, but I think that she feels a little guilty too. Her earning capacity far outpaces her husband's, and as a consequence she lets her husband run the show perhaps more than ever before.

A surrogacy fee in a city like Anand is the equivalent of ten to fifteen years' salary. So much money at one time vastly changes the quality and fabric of life for the surrogate and for her family, no matter how they spend their money. Vaina has told me she wants to be a housewife again, at home with with her children. With the money she is earning, she wants to buy her husband a taxi and send her children to a better school. I'm not sure if this will happen, but even in this very small sense, thanks to surrogacy, a woman like Vaina will take a few giant steps into the very different world of financial independence.

None of these women has ever lived without a man before. Here at the surrogacy house, surrounded only by other women and free of family, many are experiencing the joys of close friendships in new ways. None of them has ever lived with so many other women. At times, the energy in this house is like my freshman dorm in college: all giggles and excitement and women reveling in one another's company. Though they are still traditional in many senses, I see at flicker every now and again that makes me wonder how or if they'll ever find their way back completely to the world they came from.

These women don't talk much about their lives outside of the surrogate house. They sometimes mention how poor they are, but without emotion: *My son is seven, my husband's name is Ali, we are poor.* They ask nothing of me, and they don't dwell on their role as a surrogate. They simply acknowledge the facts that brought them here, and express gratitude for having been chosen for this opportunity to make their lives better and to help another, and that is that.

Usually, we talk about girl stuff, Indian fashion, Indian movies, food, how differently we dress, and of course, children. Or they ask me questions about Angelina Jolie, which always makes me laugh.

The room erupts into applause as Vaina finishes her drum solo, and I see the thrill of self-expression and appreciation register in Vaina's eyes again briefly, before she looks down once more and blushes.

"Vaina is a good drummer," I say, joining the applause. Vaina bows graciously and a little dramatically, taking her moment in the limelight, and then quickly exits stage left, handing me back the drumsticks. But something has shifted in this room. The spirit of play has overtaken us, and suddenly, everybody wants to take a turn on the drum. With every set, we laugh and laugh just as hard as we laughed the time before.

It seems like such a simple thing, being silly with a group of pregnant women and one beat-up old drum, in a room above a courtyard in a tiny village on the very edge of the modern world. But this is precisely why it's so sacred. In this moment, there is no past, no future, no words, no culture, no wealth and no poverty, no industrialized nations or developing countries. There is only the pure enjoyment of the here and now, and the endless effervescent laughter that puts its arms around all of us, and makes us one.

I want to wrap up this moment, put it in my pocket, and take it home with me so I can take it out later, unwrap it carefully, and share it with Alex and the girls at landmark moments in our lives—at christenings, bat mitzvahs, birthdays, graduations, weddings, the births of their own children—so that we as a family can remember this moment, and realize all over again how interconnected we all are, how small the world really is, and how remarkable these women were who brought my children into it.

"Is it all right if I shoot a little video?" I ask Ayisha, who interprets my request for the women. No one seems to object, so I pull out my flip camera, but the mood seems to be broken. Everyone goes back to staring at me like I'm an exhibit in a museum.

"Hello, Alex," I say, pointing the camera at my own face and waving. The waves of giggles flow again. Well, as usual, I'm clowning around. It works every time. "Hello, Alex," I say again. Then I point the camera at Vaina. "Vaina, do you want to say hello to Alex?" Vaina knows who Alex is, so she perks up immediately.

"Hello, Alex," she says, smiling and waving shyly. "Come soon."

"Hello, Alex," says Mama.

"Hello, Alex," says Asha. And then I pan the camera over the whole room and everybody waves. "Hello, Alex," they say. "Come soon!" And then we all laugh again.

I hadn't realized it would be this easy. I've been trying for weeks to force things that must unfold naturally. I see now that it has blossomed of its own accord, in its own time. Feeling connected and holding on to Vaina is as simple as cutting loose. Once again, India has taught me that the key to just about everything is to relax and breathe.

I hear a commotion in the doorway, and Vaina's three children come barreling toward me, launching themselves at their mom, smothering her with hugs and kisses. Their father barks a warning at them from the doorway. I don't understand the words he's saying, but I can tell by his tone that he's warning them to be careful with their mother. They immediately calm down and touch her very gently and cautiously.

Vaina looks radiant with her children around her. I can read in her caresses how much she misses them and how much they miss her. Vaina strokes their hair affectionately and smiles. The children are shy and polite like their mother, with the same sweet smile. Vaina has told me that her daughter wants to be a teacher, and both boys want to be astronauts.

"Do you want to play the drum?" I ask, handing one of Vaina's sons the drumsticks. He looks at his mother for permission and then grabs the sticks when she gives her consent. All three children run over to the drum and start banging away without a trace of hesitation or inhibition. The little girl perhaps most of all plays energetically and with a vibrant smile. Vaina is doing a good job with the next generation of Indian women in her household.

My bond with Vaina is very intense now; and just like the

freshman dorm or summer camp, it will change. All my relationships here are this way. Whether with the surrogates or the genetic parents, we are all intensely connected during the pregnancy and for a short time afterward, and then the relationship is over until next summer. Or maybe now, thanks to Facebook and social networking, it won't have to be. I'd love to see Caroline's babies leave the hospital. I want to see Vaina's children grow up. It won't ever be the same as it is right now.

Vaina and I will inevitably drift apart, although I wish that it were otherwise. Whatever happens, I hope that we can stay in touch somehow. But how? We live thousands of miles apart, we don't speak the same language, she doesn't have a phone, and neither she or her husband reads or writes. I would like my girls to meet her when they are older. I'd like my children to play the drums with Vaina's children while the two of us watch them from a distance, smiling contentedly, the way Vaina is smiling now.

I sit down on Vaina's bed next to her, and touch her belly.

"Why don't you take the drum home for your children?" I can see she doesn't understand me. "The drum," I say, pantomiming drumming, "for your children." Vaina understands then, smiles and holds her hands over her ears, laughing. It might be noisy, but I know that it is an appreciated gift.

"Thank you, Hadrin," she says. And then we sit quietly and watch her children play. I feel so fundamentally peaceful in this moment, and I begin to understand that while I've been trying so hard to teach Vaina what I thought she needed to know about my world, she has quietly and effortlessly been teaching me what I needed to know about myself.

I take a cue from the drum set experiment and start showing up at the surrogate house with interactive gifts. And I always include a little something that all of the surrogates can enjoy, like salty nuts to encourage salty conversation, and of course, lots and lots of chocolate. It's like a daily slumber party.

I've brought Vaina most of the things I'd brought from home for myself—mostly casual objects, a T-shirt, a ring I'd picked up at a San Francisco art fair years before, just tokens to let her know I was thinking about her. Few of the gifts were valuable, though I did once give her a diamond bracelet that I'd bought for myself some years ago, and another bracelet that had belonged to Alex's grandmother. It felt natural to give her this jewelry; she is family now. Vaina wore this jewelry once, and then I never saw it again. I never asked what happened to the bracelets. They are hers now, and it is none of my business.

This morning, I look in my suitcase and realize that I've just about run out of American gifts. I remember that Vaina has told me that she likes my makeup, so I grab my cosmetics kit and dash out the door, too late, as usual, to beat the morning rush. I always think that the minute I turn my back, something will happen to Vaina that I should be present for. I live in a constant state of readiness.

Today is a school day, so as I approach the surrogate house, the women are just finishing English class. Vaina is not with them. She's still on bed rest, restricted to her room, so I race upstairs.

"How are you feeling today?" I ask her. Our vocabulary is very limited and requires visual aids, but I've learned that what is said matters less than how it's said. Just being here, holding Vaina's hand, matters more to both of us than the words.

"Tired today," she says. "Hi, Alex, California, I like San Francisco, I like New York," says Vaina, looking very proud of herself. I laugh. It appears the English Vaina is learning has been targeted to my life.

"Very good," I say, noticing that she looks a little pale today. *"Kemm cho, aavjo. Tame kya cho!"* I say, repeating the few essential Gujarati words I've learned for *hello, good-bye,* and *give me some water quick!* Vaina laughs and hands me a glass of water.

"I brought a present for you," I tell her, and she smiles excitedly. She does this every time I bring her anything, grapes or diamonds; it all gets the same smile. It matters less what I give; Vaina truly does care more about the thought behind the gift. I unzip my makeup case and start putting the little tubes and jars in her lap. She looks a little mystified at the compacts and brushes. It's one of Vaina's signature looks, that says, *Thank you but what the hell is this stuff?* That expression of hers is a big part of the fun.

I open my powder and blush and my contouring brush, and start applying it to Vaina's face. A few of the younger surrogates gather around, intrigued, to watch what I'm doing, and I suspect to giggle at me a little bit. I'm a good sport in the surrogate house, but I also know that they are very impressed and a little jealous that I spend so much time with Vaina. Many of them are pregnant with the babies of couples whom they won't even meet until the birth.

There are lots of Western cosmetics available in India, so it's not really the products themselves that are interesting to these women. It's the colors that are strange and exotic, and the way I apply them. The concept of beauty and the cosmetics industry in India is an interesting mix. On the one hand, there is a focus on being natural and ayurvedic, in terms of alternative medicine and balance. Indian women use yogurt to moisturize the skin, and stress the importance of inner peace in every beauty regimen. They value the simple and the unadorned. On the other hand, coexisting right alongside these minimalist, health-based cosmetic traditions, is the fact that Indian women, by Western standards, literally pile on makeup for events and traditional gatherings. They wear a thick black eyeliner called kohl, which is a pigment dye and very dark, with a lot of dramatic vibrant eye shadow and bright, bright lipstick. They also wear elaborate jewelry and, for married women, a red dot between their eyes, called a *bindhi*.

Both looks are very different from the minimalist, natural look I am creating for Vaina. When I'm done, Vaina looks at herself in the mirror and seems pleased with her reflection, if a little disappointed, as the colors are so neutral. I can tell the other women are curious, and so the rest of the afternoon is taken up with eye shadow and lip gloss and questions about Angelina Jolie. It appears that girl talk, just like music, is a universal language.

❄︎⊱❄︎⊰❄︎

The next morning I arrive at the clinic early because Vaina has a sonogram scheduled. I'm dying of anticipation to see how much my babies have grown in the last week. But when I arrive at the clinic to meet Vaina to go into town for the procedure, I find Dr. Patel waiting for me by the front desk.

"Vaina is bleeding," she says to me. The blood drains from my face and my palms are instantly clammy.

"Is that bad?" I ask. "What's wrong?" My fingers are like ice. I think my circulation has stopped dead in its tracks.

"No reason to worry," says Dr. Patel in that way she has that reminds and reassures you that she's got everything under control, even if I suspect that sometimes this isn't always the case.

"The bleeding means that the babies are ready to be born. We are cutting the stitch today."

"But it's still three and a half weeks early!" I say.

"They are ready," she says again. "Babies in India are often born at thirty-six weeks, especially twins. It's very common. I think they are just too excited to jump into life and can't wait any longer. "

"So everything's okay?" I say, thinking, *Honestly, Adrienne, can you be a bit more articulate?* At this moment, I can barely think straight. Nothing else matters but Dr. Patel's answer.

"Everything's okay," says Dr. Patel, and puts her arm around me for a moment. She is not often physically affectionate, so I'm touched. "Everything is just fine unless you've changed your mind about wanting to be a mom."

I look at Dr. Patel, and I can tell I'm about to burst into tears. I am speechless. I've been waiting for this moment for what feels like centuries, but now that it's finally arrived, I'm completely knocked for a loop. I no longer feel numb; instead, I'm hyperemotional. Each emotion and thought—joy, terror, should I still give Vaina her gift?—is hitting me with a blazing intensity. Dr. Patel can see that I am awash in a flood of feelings I can't express, and focuses me on the business at hand. It's one of the many things that makes her so good at her job.

"Better call Alex," she says to me, "and tell him to book a flight. He's about to become a father."

chapter 13

I'm dreaming about the girls, my girls. I'm holding them both for the very first time. I'm staring at them, trying to memorize their faces, as if they will disappear at any moment and I'll be able to hold them only in memory. I don't want to pull my eyes away, not even to eat or sleep. Then I realize I have the rest of my life to learn these faces; to watch their expressions as they take in the vast variety of the world for the very first time. I'll watch these faces change from newborn babies to intrepid toddlers to petulant teenagers. I will know these faces until the day I die.

I reach out and stroke their little faces for the first time. They are so soft, and so perfectly pink. The girls open their eyes and look at me. "I'm your mommy," I tell them, and it seems to me that they understand. "I'm your mom, and I love you very much, Emma and India."

I wake up with a start. After nine months of playing obsessive alphabet games trying to come up with names that begin with *A*, I realize my babies' names don't start with *A* at all. They're Emma and India, *E* and *I*. Emma after a dear friend who looked and sounded like an angel to me, and India, to remind us of where it all began. Of course those are their names. Why hadn't I known this all along? Maybe if I had been carrying them, I would have.

It's no wonder my imagination is doing jumping jacks this morning. Tomorrow or the day after will be Emma and India's birth day. And Alex will be here to share it with us! Vaina's bleeding indicated that it was time for her to begin labor, which is what she has been doing for the last six hours. I returned home to the hotel to rest for a bit and prepare myself.

There is so much to get ready for, even though I've been doing nothing but preparing for months. There are baby clothes and toys and cribs and a bassinet with mosquito netting piled up in the corner of my hospitality suite. That symbolic and completely neglected pile had begun to get a little depressing, just sitting there, unused, and completely disorganized, waiting, the same way I was. But it won't be much longer now.

I walk over to the pile and start to pick through the onesies and rattles, trying to put some order into a piledup life that has not begun yet. Then the phone rings. Since I've been in India, it feels as if the phone only rings when there's an emergency. "Hello?" I say, bracing myself.

"Vaina is ready to give birth," Dr. Patel says with characteristic brevity. "We are doing a Csection now as she is bleeding a lot, and one of the babies is breeched. Please get here in the next fifteen to twenty minutes." And then she hangs up, no doubt because she is sprinting to the delivery room. I have a vision of her disappearing into a doorway in a flutter of blue silk, black braids, and efficiency.

Vaina is ready to give birth. Vaina's in labor, right now, in real time. I have to be there in fifteen or twenty minutes. I have to get to the hospital. My heart is pounding, my legs are immobilized. I haven't moved one inch toward the door. Then I realize Alex won't be here for two more days. I call him, only to get his voice mail.

"Alex," I say, "Vaina's giving birth. I'm headed to the hospital. I'll call you from the delivery room. And, Alex, I love you. Oh my God, this is it! I love you. Okay, I'll call you from there."

I realize my generally razor-sharp verbal communication skills have completely disintegrated in the blink of an eye. Who cares? Suddenly, my adrenal glands turn on like somebody's just thrown a switch and flooded my system with rocket fuel. I jump up and go running into the streets. A rickshaw pulls over and I tell the driver to take me to the clinic, quick! Saying "quick" to a cab driver is roughly the equivalent of saying, *I'm new in town, do with me what you will*. Anybody who has been in Anand for any amount of time realizes that there is no such thing as "quick."

I'm texting Alex like a maniac as I make my way through the traffic. The heat and excitement are battling for control over my senses, but everything seems drowsy and just slightly out of focus. The landscape of the moment no longer surrounds me but seems to shimmer in the distance, like it's all a mirage. We drive past all my personal Anand landmarks, and it's like I'm seeing them in a whole new light. I pass the nut stand where I buy Vaina's almonds each day, the bazaar where I found the drum set, the vegetarian Pizza Hut, the Ice Palace, Café Coffee, the hotel where I stayed the first time I came here for IVF, before Abhi transported me to the glamorous Hotel Laksh. I pass by the holy cows, the mud-caked camels, the rattling trucks filled with bright Rajasthan embroidered cotton, and the stalls filled with bananas and jasmine, roses, and piquant spices of every color.

They appear to me suddenly as I suspect they will appear in memory—sun-kissed, symbolic, sentimental. I remember how exotic this all appeared to me when I first arrived, and marvel at how familiar these images have become. I wonder what it will be like when I'm back in San Francisco. Will my hometown now seem as exotic and strange to me as the streets of Anand once did? Or will it seem dull and impersonal by comparison? This experience has lifted me up out of my normal milieu, and once it sets me back down again, I wonder, will anything ever seem the same as it was before?

I think, *This is part of becoming a mom.* Your context changes forever. Your world, the view through which you perceive everything, will now include two other people, inextricably linked to you, as if by an invisible thread, for the rest of your life. I wonder, will I feel this way even though I haven't carried my babies? Will Vaina feel this way, because she has? Or will she, like Ahmed said in Dr. Patel's book, never give us a second thought after the girls are born? Will they remember her?

It is with my head racing through these complex and unanswerable questions that I finally arrive at the clinic. The second I open the door, the nurse with the movie star smile grabs me and pulls me toward the delivery suite waiting room. I sit down to dial Alex.

"Hi, my love," I whisper, not wanting to disturb the surgically sacred atmosphere of the place. I feel like I'm in a library, or a church. Thankfully, now I have Alex on the line. "They're coming to get me so I'm putting you on speakerphone."

Vaina's husband is sitting next to me in the waiting room. He looks almost as excited as I am, but for very different reasons. He gets to have his wife back. And for him, I think, perhaps too cynically, today is payday. I shouldn't be hard on him. After all, it's payday for me too. I put my hand on his shoulder briefly and he smiles uncomfortably. A nurse enters and puts a surgical gown over my shoulders, claps a mask and a cap on my head, and before I know it, I'm being pushed through the swinging doors into the operating theater, which is when I come face-to-face with my daughter Emma, who has just that moment been born.

I know that she is Emma because she is as pink as an English tea rose, while India, who follows right behind her, is dark-skinned and exotic-looking. Alex hears India and Emma cry for the very first time, just as I do. I hear Alex start to cry right along with them. I, who have been operating with my shields completely down, now suddenly feel numb again. It will take some time before the heartaches of the past recede and I can greet the unknown without fear.

I know this is one of the defining moments of my lifetime, and that I'll want to relive it over and over again. I'm concentrating on every tiny detail so that I can tell the girls and Alex all about it for years to come.

This is not the softly lit, blissful delivery room scene that I had dreamed of. I wasn't standing by Vaina's side holding her hand and coaching her through labor. Alex wasn't next to me cheering us on. My babies do not look like two cute, squeaky-clean little angels wrapped in fuzzy pink blankets. Instead, they are wriggling, four-pound little creatures who are at the moment covered in blood and placenta and squalling to beat the band. Alex is sobbing over speakerphone. And Dr. Patel is standing right in front of me, with unbilical cords in her hands. Although I am a doctor's daughter, I am not a good sport when it comes to the sight of blood, let alone an entire lower GI system. I start to go weak in the knees.

Then I look down at Vaina, who is conscious and beaming up at me with such pride that my heart melts. She looks so vulnerable, and yet so strong. I'm supposed to be the strong partner in this process, and she needs me to tell her what an amazing, incredible thing she has done. I take a deep breath, get my legs back underneath me, bend down and kiss Vaina on the forehead. All ten doctors and nurses in the delivery room erupt in loud cheers and applause, a spontaneous celebration of life that I know I will remember forever. And in this moment I realize that I wouldn't have traded this completely chaotic, and slightly less than sanitary experience, for the fanciest hospital in Beverly Hills. This is everything that I could have ever hoped for, and more.

"Alex," I say, looking at our daughters, and then at the doctors and nurses who are smiling and cheering all around me, "they're so beautiful. Everyone is so beautiful." And then, finally, I start to cry tears of joy and enormous relief. It's over. And I'm not numb anymore.

❋❀❋❀❋

But of course, as anyone knows who has had a baby, birth isn't an end of the terror that is motherhood, it's only the beginning. A few hours later, the babies are transferred to the emergency room at the NICU in Anand. The girls are healthy but a bit small, at only four pounds each. They also have jaundice, so they have been put in incubators for twenty-four hours. I know jaundice is common, I had it myself as a child, but seeing them so tiny under those bright lights breaks my heart. The nurse tells me that a surrogate is staying with them all night to breast-feed them and for some reason, I burst into tears. I wish Alex were here to help me deal with all of this. But it's only Tuesday, and Alex won't be here until Thursday.

The next day, the babies are sent back to the clinic, where they'll stay so they can breast-feed for as long as possible with another surrogate who has been hired for this purpose. While this seems strange to me every time I think about it, it really does make sense. I feel good about this decision. I'm glad that

Emma and India will have the advantages of breast-feeding. And there are women at the clinic who know what they're doing when it comes to babies.

I am so happy that I had my babies in India, with all of these wonderful, caring people surrounding me. If I had had the babies in the United States, I feel for some reason that I would have been sucked in by baby consumerism and made my decisions based on the decisions other people were making, instead of being guided my own better instincts. Since I am here, away from the pressures of my own culture, family, and friends, I can learn to be a new parent on my own, without any societal pressure or parenting magazines to tell me that I should do things a certain way.

In India, there won't be anyone around to tell me that I'm evil for not breast-feeding, or what products I have to buy, or what type of clothing the babies should be wearing, or which diaper is most absorbent and still eco-friendly. There are no rules here, except to be kind and to watch and appreciate the miracle of these two little beings growing and thriving.

While I'd love to bring them home this instant, I don't exactly have a home to bring them to. I have a convenience suite, where there are bassinets and baby clothes and baby bottles and sterilizers all lying in a jumbled heap by my bed. It's hardly a dream nursery, and I certainly don't feel ready to take on two brand-new babies in a convenience suite in the Hotel Laksh without my husband here to help me. This is going to take some getting used to.

And the secret truth is, I still worry about whether I'm ready to be a mother. I don't *feel* like a mother yet. What's a mother supposed to feel like, anyway? I wish that my mother were here to tell me what is normal, what is to be expected. My heart is bursting at the mere thought of being a mom to these two perfect healthy bundles of joy, and yet, still a daughter myself, I desperately wish my own mom were here, to help me and tell me what she knows about how to navigate this new terrain. Then I remember that my mother taught me to be independent, and that I can do whatever I set my mind to. And I realize too that she has already taught me what I need to know about being a good mother, through the way she mothered me. Suddenly I feel my mom all around me—I've gotten the message, and I can feel her love, just as if she were here in the room with me.

I decide to stay at the clinic for a few nights. When I see Vaina for the first time since the birth, she looks weak and tired from the C-section. She had given birth to her own twin boys naturally, so I feel terrible that she had to go through this to bring my twins into the world. A ray of sunlight shines through the window illuminating India's face. She gurgles and cries a little, and Vaina opens her eyes and smiles at me. She doesn't look at India. I put the flowers I've brought her on the table by her bed. It seems like such a meager offering after what she's just done for me.

"Pretty," she says, "pretty, Hadrin. The babies are pretty too." And she smiles. I take her hand. But I can tell she doesn't really think the babies are all that pretty. She looks at them like they are something foreign, not connected to her at all.

"The babies are beautiful," I say, picking up Emma and stroking her cheek. "You did a wonderful job, Vaina. How can I ever thank you?" I feel overwhelmed with emotion and start getting all teary again. Vaina looks like she's in pain, and I put India back in her bassinet.

"How are you feeling?" I ask.

"Good. A little tired." She rubs her belly, revealing the fresh scar across her abdomen. I want to let her know that we both have scars from trying to bring babies into the world. I want to remind her that her sacrifice was worthwhile, and remind my-self that I too had suffered trying to carry my own children. I pull up my dress and pull down the waist of my underwear to show her my scar. It's smaller, and in time, mine has faded to white while Vaina's is still an angry red. She looks at my belly and immediately tears up. She squeezes my hand. She under-stands. Through these many months, without our even realiz-ing it, we have invented our own language. It's a language of shared joy and love and pain, too. It's a lexicon that mothers everywhere understand, without uttering a word.

Just then, Vaina's husband walks into the room, and sees me standing by his wife's bed with my dress up around my waist. He is absolutely mortified and turns quickly on his heel and walks back down the stairs. Vaina's and my tears turn immedi-ately to giggles, and we hold hands, realizing that our friendship, and what we have just created together, has managed to bridge two worlds that rarely collide. We are engaged in something very special and rare.

※·ᵒ·❀·ᵒ·※

The next two days pass in a sleepless whirlwind. The bed in the clinic is even more uncomfortable than the bed in the hotel, which I wouldn't have thought possible. I'm happy to be so close to Vaina and the girls. I don't feel like a mother yet, but I'm getting to know my daughters. I stare at them, trying to memorize their faces and learn what lies beneath. I can al-ready see how different they are from each other and from me and Alex. Such distinct personalities and they are only two days old.

I remember the people back home who asked me if I was going to have brown babies because I was using an Indian sur-rogate; or who scolded me for being unethical and exploiting the wombs of disadvantaged women. Those concerns ring hollow now, in the wake of the miracle of cooperation I am witnessing every day as we at the surrogate house collectively care for my babies. For perhaps the first time in my life, I couldn't care less what anybody else thinks. I know that I've made the right decision.

This experience has taught me to trust my instincts and my ability to nurture my own children. This country gave me refuge after I lost my mother and lost my way, and now it has given me direction and purpose. India has taught me that things in general and babies in particular want to grow, and will if you let them. This country has given me the confidence to know with certainty that I'm a good mother, and that my decisions are fine.

❈❀❀❀❈

The twins are growing slowly. They both lost a bit of weight after delivery. They look nothing alike—it is amazing! Emma is serene and peaceful, and India is wild and already has a much bigger personality. The breast-feeding is not coming easily. Emma appears to be growing more quickly and eats well, but India is very thin and screams constantly. Dr. Patel is examining them this morning, and as soon as she sees India she looks at me, very alarmed. This is unusual. I don't think I've ever seen her flustered.

"Adrienne," she said to me, "you have to bring in a pediatrician. There is something wrong with India. She's not thriving."

I feel immediate panic. Why is Dr. Patel so upset? Babies are supposed to cry, aren't they?

"Of course, whatever you think," I say. "But, who should we call?"

"I know a very good man in town; I'll put in a call for you. We'll want him right away. We must get to the bottom of this," she says, and then disappears into a procedure room to deal with her usual throng of impatiently waiting patients.

I pick up the babies and go to visit Vaina. I'm feeling incredible guilt that I didn't know that India was sick. Why didn't I know that something was wrong? As her mother, shouldn't I have known this first? Shouldn't I have sensed this and acted before having to be told?

Vaina looks exhausted but smiles at me as I come into the room. India, mercifully, stops crying and falls asleep. Just then, I hear a soft knock on the door, and look up to see Alex, beaming at me, taking in the faces of his daughters for the very first time.

"Alex!" I say a little too loudly. India wakes up and immediately begins to cry. I throw my arms around him. I don't think that I've ever been so happy to see anybody in my life. "Thank God you're here."

"Hi, little pugees." Already beginning his habit of creating new nicknames on the spot, Alex kisses India and Emma on their little furrowed foreheads. "Adrienne, they're so little and cute. They're just beautiful. Just like their mommy." I take Emma and India, and Alex puts his arms around all of us and for the first time we embrace as a family. It is a perfect moment, until India starts to cry fitfully again and I have to tell Alex what is going on.

"Something's wrong with India," I blurt out, and all the worry instantly appears on my face. "Dr. Patel doesn't know what the problem is so they're bringing in a pediatrician."

"Oh, no, is it serious?" says Alex, having his first flirtation with parental panic. I am instantly reassured; it will be nice to share some of the terror that these first few days inevitably entail. The stakes are so high now, and Alex has always been better than I am in a crisis.

"I guess we'll find out," I say. I put Emma in Alex's arms

then and he stands there, a twin on each elbow, with a great big dad grin on his face, but I can see that he's overwhelmed. He's just flown eight thousand miles to meet his daughters for the first time, and reunite with his wife, and he finds me standing next to our exhausted-looking surrogate, with a screaming underweight child in my arms.

Fortunately, the panic I feel at not knowing what is wrong with my daughter is short-lived. The pediatrician arrives just after midnight in a ubiquitous white lab coat, a symbol of reassurance the world over. The doctor examines both babies, then places the tip of his pinky in India's mouth and she suckles frantically.

"So, what is it?" I ask, almost not wanting to know the answer.

"This baby is hungry," he proudly announces. "Wean them both from the breast milk and move on to formula. They will be fine. Just make sure they eat," he says emphatically, shaking our hands officiously and then hurrying off to talk to Dr. Patel. Bottles of formula are quickly secured and bottles prepared. Both twins eat hungrily and the crying, mercifully, stops.

Alex and I look at each other, and then burst out laughing from pure relief and fall into each other's arms. We are going to be okay. The bottom was not going to fall out. We are, at last, a family.

Making the switch from breast-feeding at the clinic to formula is a bigger proposition than we had imagined. I have been shuttling back and forth to the clinic at all hours of the night bringing formula, as they don't have any at the clinic. Formula is not included in the package, and it's difficult to find in Anand. The security guard usually gives me a ride on his motorcycle and will never accept money from me. He just says he wants God to be with me.

At midnight two nights ago, we needed to get a taxi for our

second bottle of formula from the clinic and I wanted Alex to go to sleep before he fell over from exhaustion, but he insisted on coming. The challenge, of course, is that Anand isn't exactly a party town. The Muslims and Hindus here do not go out past nine at night, so there were no taxis or rickshaws in sight. Then, out of nowhere, two huge white horses appear, pulling a gold, and silver-enameled carriage on its way back from a wedding ceremony. It was straight out of a fairy tale. We asked the driver if we could hitch a ride, he said yes, and we climbed on in. It was so magical and unbelievable and amusing, as the locals understandably thought we were newlyweds. We thought that my mom must have arranged this regal ride in celebration of all of us being together.

The next morning, we go to see another pediatrician. He is also called Dr. Patel, and he is lovely. He used to work in Manhattan, so his English is fluid and easy to understand. He is also cute, and all the kids at the clinic love him. He confirms that now that they're eating and the jaundice has cleared up, everything is looking good with the babies. We now have the babies with us at the hotel full-time. We thought it might be too soon to take them out of the clinic, but the pediatrician says that this is the best course of action. We have set up a whole system for bottle sterilization, which is nothing short of epic, but we are managing well and loving our new role as parents of twin baby girls.

Sometimes at the clinic in secret I let the babies nurse from what I have come to refer to as a breast pacifier. I'm not producing milk, obviously, but I still want a tiny bit of that feeling, that connection to their infants, that nursing mothers have when they breast-feed. So I created my own system for creating that bond. It seems to calm the babies, and it makes me feel closer to them as well. I'm going to tell Alex what I'm doing tonight. He has been joking that my breasts look bigger since the girls were born. Maybe this is why.

Alex is a natural in his new role. It's incredible. He actually loves changing diapers and preparing formula. There is nothing cuter than a man feeding his daughter her bottle. He is taking so many notes and just loves being around the girls. We are having so much fun together, and we just can't stop staring at our daughters as they lie next to each other.

This has been such a long, sometimes exhilarating and sometimes exhausting journey, and now that we have arrived at our happily ever after, I wouldn't change a single second of it. But nobody told me that having twins was going to be so much work!

chapter 14

Alex will be going home soon to pick up the documents we'll need to get exit visas, since nobody ever told us we were going to need a copy of our marriage license to get out of the country, and we have hired a nurse, Kristi, who is a godsend. Of course, Abhi introduced us to her, as Abhi introduces us to just about everyone and everything that we find we need in Anand. Kristi is probably in her late sixties and is always dressed in a perfect sari. She loves her tea, dal, her family photographs, almonds, and her Bible. Since Kristi moved in with us, our environment is filled with the sounds of soft Gujarati lullabies that she sings to the babies every morning and every night.

She is a soft soul with a beautiful spirit, and she is very religious, a Pentecostal minister's wife, which must be difficult, as she lives in a Muslim village. Kristi loves talking about God and always says to me, "God bless you, and God bless Hemma and India." She also says, "Jesus is my savior." Her husband blesses the babies a few times a week in heavy prayer and chanting. The only word I can make out is always the same, "Jesus, Jesus, Jesus." The all-pervasive Christianity alarmed me at first, as I am Jewish and not accustomed to the liturgy surrounding me at every waking moment, but as time goes by, I decide to accept the blessings in the spirit in which they are intended.

It's incredible how close Kristi and I have become through the simple acceptance of each other's beliefs and lifestyles and caring for the children. Sometimes I grab her Bible for a quick moment and hold it, feel it, look at the words, and they start to mean something to me because Kristi means something to me. Because of the language barrier, conversation isn't exactly stimulating but it doesn't have to be. Sometimes a quick smile is all we need. Between her Bible and my books and the babies the days go by very quickly.

We had many communication issues at the beginning—from diaper changes to bottle feeding, to sleeping, were the babies too warm, too cold—and would call Abhi three or four times a day to translate. Abhi is so calm and patient, always helping us with translation and being so friendly. Then, just as I had with Vaina, I started to find ways to communicate without a translator, without words, and we did pretty well on our own after that.

Last night, Alex and I smuggled a little port wine and two chairs up to the roof. It was so lovely to be together, watching the sun set next to the tobacco and banana fields . . . until I walked to the other side of the roof and discovered a chicken slaughterhouse. I was surprised that there was a slaughterhouse so near the hotel, when I'd been trying in vain to eat something other than rice and lentils for four months, but it explained why there was such a shortage of eggs; they killed almost all the chickens. It was a bit different than the romantic evening alone I had envisioned. One moment, banana fields, soft kisses, and port; the next, a slaughterhouse filled with terrified chickens.

Yet, despite all the sometimes jarring juxtapositions, I've grown to love this country. In fact, I've become so attached to India that Alex is worried I will stay here with the girls and never go back! I want this place to be always in my life, and I want to stay connected to all the kind people here who have touched my heart, made me laugh and think, and I want to be the best person possible professionally and personally. The water, the food, the climate: none of it fazes me anymore. I feel happy to be here—everything feels just right.

Alex says when he sees me with the babies, he feels proud of us as a couple. We made so many sacrifices for this life, and finally things seem to be falling into place for us.

Though he missed me while I was living here, he also understands and values my experience here. He is happy that I was by Vaina's side during her last weeks of pregnancy. He knows how profound it was for me to feel the babies kick, to see the sonograms, to bond with the woman who was carrying our children, and I think he understands that because of this time in India, I don't feel that I missed out on the experience of being pregnant. I never, ever thought the word *happy* would be associated with any of my pregnancies, that I'd ever be grateful for those terrible experiences in San Francisco.

Our marriage has deepened. It's become more profound because we have a shared responsibility now. When we were at lunch the other day, we found ourselves mixing bottles for the girls right at the table in the middle of the restaurant, completely unaware of everybody around us. We caught ourselves acting like all the zoned-out parents we'd seen thousands of times before, the ones we always saw and wondered if that would ever be us. Now we were actually those people, the ones we had envied for so long. I caught Alex's eye. Our lives are changing right now, and they will never be the same.

Sometimes I wonder if having twins should even be allowed. There is just so much work involved. Even with Kristi, I often feel outnumbered. Sterilizing bottles, mixing formula, running to pediatrician appointments, washing dirty clothes, changing diapers, putting them down for naps, getting them up from naps, keeping them cool and mosquito free: it's like a merry-go-round. We can never keep up with it all, but with Kristi, it's easier, especially if I multitask. This morning, I brushed my teeth with one hand, checked email with one finger, and gave Emma a tummy massage with my foot. They are two and a half weeks old now, and our pediatrician here tells me that this should be the easy part!

Alex and I are getting our routine down pat. Eat, burp, diaper change, sleep. Repeat. It sounds easy, but really, it's quite involved. Just to prepare formula we have to scrub the bottles inside and out with local water and dishwasher detergent. Then we rinse them with bottled water. Then we put them in the steam sterilizer to kill any residual germs. Then we rinse with bottled water again, and finally fill them with formula. We have to make three bottles per child per night, and because the formula is stable for only a few hours, the bottles have to be refrigerated. Steady temperature of any kind is never a simple thing in Anand, because the power grid is unstable, so when the power fails, I have to throw out the prepared formula and make new batches, but I have to wait until the power returns before I can sterilize the bottles, and if the girls want to be fed before the power returns, their screams wake everyone in the hotel. I was so focused on getting through the pregnancy that I had never thought about the ritualistic and surgically precise exercises I'd have to engage in to prevent our babies from getting dysentery. To say that we are constantly on our toes is an understatement.

Last night, I spoke on Skype with our U.S. pediatrician. She is a Stanford graduate with about a hundred other degrees and accolades after her name. She quickly reminded me about all the things I *should* be doing, like giving the babies special vitamin drops and swapping the formula we are using for something that will be easier for them to digest. By the time I hung up, I felt like I needed a PhD just to care for my newborns.

Of course, in India they don't sell the kind of formula our California pediatrician recommended, and of course she's told us that it's the one and only formula the girls should have. I will have to ask friends and relations to literally scour the world for cans of the stuff, which they then have to shuttle in by plane because it would cost over five hundred dollars to ship it. Needless to say, Anand does not have a FedEx office.

Our phone call reminded me of what it may feel like to be a new mom back home; the constant third-party instructions, expectations, second-guessing and guilt about whether or not I'm a good mom will begin. I appreciate all of her advice and I'm glad I touched base, but my time in India has enabled me to follow my own instincts and to be comfortable with that. For that sense of confidence, I will always be thankful. By contrast, in India, the doctors and older women will tell you to do three things: hold your baby, feed your baby, and change her diaper. That is the Indian prescription. The rest is up to God.

Despite all the bottle steaming and formula mixing, life is wonderful. My future has finally arrived. Time no longer drips like molasses on a cold January day. Now, I relish the slow passage of time. Of all things, I want each moment to pass more slowly, so I can properly savor what they are like at ten days old, or two weeks, or three weeks. Now that the girls have been born, I'm finally in step with the slower pace of Indian life. and just spend hours staring at the girls, happy to just sit and watch them grow.

There is still the issue of exit visas, which Alyssa has warned me can be difficult.

Slowly, I'm saying good-bye to all the familiar sights and

sounds and smells of this wonderful country, and to my home away from home, the crazy Hotel Laksh.

My father called to say he hit the lottery and found four big cans of our formula at a health food store in Beverly Hills, so he's flying in to replenish our stash personally—and meet his granddaughters—next week. I can't believe he's coming. My father never goes anywhere unless they have at least five four-star restaurants, the *New York Times,* and three world-renowned cultural institutions within walking distance of his hotel. I suspect Anand and the Hotel Laksh may be a bit below his expectations, but I'm so looking forward to seeing him, and I'm thrilled that he'll meet his granddaughters for the first time in their birthplace, India.

Ever since I became a mother, I've been thinking of my own. After so many months of roller-coaster emotions, I expected to feel stable now that the girls are here. Instead, I miss my mother with a ferocity that knocks the wind out of me. I had no idea that loss would feel as torturous and fresh and raw as it does. Some days, I feel deeply wounded without her or simply miss her, but most of the time, I'm frustrated that she never got to have these two little souls in her life, and they'll never have a relationship with her that is independent. They'll only get to know their grandmother through my stories, my sister's memories, and my father's family pictures.

I see so much of my mom in Emma's face. Her eyes are the same color and shape as my mother's and with that signature twinkle that says, *Go ahead, I dare you!* She also has a similar skin tone and pouty lips like my mom did. India looks more like Alex's side of the family, but India too has the Carol Arieff twinkle whenever she laughs.

Alex and I have decided we should move to Ahmedabad with the girls so that we can be closer to the state capital when it's time to go for our exit visas. Fatima, the girl at the front desk whom I've become friendly with, thinks she is moving to California with us. I made a lighthearted joke one day about her coming back home with us, and she jumped at the idea. She now wants to postpone her plans to join a convent, and to give up purity for God in favor of going to the beach. I told her that God is more fun than the beach, but she doesn't seem convinced.

I also have to say good-bye to Vaina.

Everyone told me that as soon as the baby is born, you realize you and your surrogate are starting to separate, but I had thought that Vaina and I might be different. We are not. The birth was difficult for her, as were the months and months away from her family. She is ready to go home. After months and months of waiting, I'm finally a mom. Still, it's a difficult adjustment. I haven't gone a single day without seeing her since I arrived all those months ago. It's hard to imagine a time when my days weren't defined and shaped by my daily visits with Vaina. What will it be like when our visits stop? How will I feel when Vaina disappears back into the morning Gujarati mist from whence she emerged nine months ago?

I wish we could stay connected, but I have no idea how Vaina and I would even keep in touch. She lives in a remote village, and Dr. Patel has already told me that if I want to get news to Vaina, I should do so only through the clinic. Dr. Patel discourages surrogates and couples from continuing their relationships. This is not what the journey is about, as far as she is concerned. Maintaining a close relationship, as in an open adoption, poses potential risks for surrogates and parents alike. I understand all this. I know in my head that the time has come for us to separate, that it's the right thing to do. I see the wisdom in this. It's time for Alex, Emma, India, and me to start to live our lives together, as a family.

"Good morning," says Abhi, entering the room after knock‑ing briefly and getting no answer. He is lighting up the room with his smile, as usual. I will be sad to say good‑bye to Abhi as well, even though we had at times butted heads. "Are you ready to go to the clinic now?" The time has finally come.

I put some cash in an envelope, grab a bunch of Toblerone bars, the San Francisco Giants caps Alex has brought for Vaina's children, and a brand‑new cell phone, kiss the girls, who are safe in Kristi's arms, and we head out the door. And of course, on the one day when I'm not in a hurry to arrive at the clinic, and am, in fact, dreading the moment of arrival, there is no traffic and we get there in record time.

"Are you okay, my love?" Alex asks me; I'm acting like a cat on a hot tin roof.

"I'll be fine," I say, because I know ultimately that I will be. "But if it's okay, I'd like to go up alone."

"No problem," Alex says, and kisses me. "I'll go and say hello to Hitesh and then go be with the girls until you're done."

Alex heads off in the direction of the front desk, and I walk those familiar stairs up to the surrogate room for the very last time. I enter the room, and see Vaina sitting on her bed by the window. Her bags are packed and stacked at the foot of the bed, ready to go. Her children are all around her, laughing and play‑ing excitedly because their mom is coming back to them. They leave for their village this afternoon. She smiles at me in that way she always has, instantly telling me she has missed me and is happy to see me.

I sit next to her on the bed and take her hand as I always do. But everything feels different and unfamiliar today. Our body language is awkward. We both know this is good‑bye, and now that the time has come for us to go our separate ways and re‑

turn to our lives, we are as ill at ease as if we're meeting for the very first time.

"Are you happy to be going home?" Ayisha interprets for me.

"Yes, happy to see my children, my husband," Vaina says, and I smile. Me too, I think. I pull out the envelope and give it to her. She doesn't look inside, but she knows what's there and smiles politely.

"Thank you, Hadrin," she says gracefully and slips the envelope into her purse. I give the caps to the children, and put the last one on Vaina's head. She and the other surrogates laugh. It reminds me of that wonderful day when we laughed for hours over the beat-up drum. I want to find some way to maintain contact, I want there to be a thread that still physically connects us, even though we will be worlds apart.

"I've brought you a cell phone," I say, pulling out the phone and giving it to her. She looks at it with delight. "I've programmed my number in it, so you can call me anytime. If you ever need anything, you just call me," I say, and the translator relays what I'm saying. Of course, we wouldn't have Ayisha translating for us if we ever do speak on the phone, but if Vaina ever hit my number on her speed dial, just hearing her laugh would be enough.

Vaina smiles and puts the cell phone down and then picks up her purse to look for something. She draws out two beautifully interwoven strands of thread. They are different shades of red, Vaina's favorite color. She hands the strands to me.

"For the girls," she says. Through the interpreter, Vaina explains that these are sacred threads, given to her by her Hindu best friend when she was just a girl. She explains to me that in her friend's tradition, a sacred thread is given to a baby on the day she is born, so that no matter where life takes her, she will always be attached to her mother. She tells me that her friend gave her these threads when she left the village, so they would always stay connected at the heart. Now she presses these same threads into my hand, and says to me in English, "Now these threads will always connect us."

Tears splash down my cheeks. "I will miss you," says Vaina, and hugs me. There is no way that this is the end of our story, that I will have to say good-bye to this woman forever. I will find a way to see her again, somehow.

"I will see you soon, my angel," I say helplessly.

"I will miss you," Vaina says again.

"I will miss you too," I say, we hug and kiss one last time, and then I force myself to stand up, march out of the door, and I cry all the way home. Vaina had become more than a surrogate, she had become a friend, and leaving her left me with an empty feeling inside, a sense of loss, because I knew that although we would always be connected through the girls, things would never be the same between us again.

chapter 15

Tomorrow the twins will be three weeks old. It is Easter week, end, which I didn't think would be observed, because there are so few Christians in this part of India. But people have been dropping by our hotel room to greet the babies and deliver a prayer. It is an Easter tradition here to bless babies. "Every child is a gift from God," they say, or "Praise the Lord, the children are a miracle." If they only knew how much of a miracle India and Emma really are!

My father arrived in Ahmedabad last week, which was a wonderful break after the sadness of separating from Vaina. It was so incredible to see him. He got off the plane loaded loaded down with gifts and pj's and onesies and loads of formula. Watching his face when he laid eyes on his granddaughters for the first time was a moment I will never forget. My dad immediately burst into tears. He kept saying over and over again how beautiful the girls were, each in their own way. How did I get so lucky to have such an adorable father?

My dad seemed to have inexhaustible patience for the girls, which is going to come in handy down the line, I have a feeling! He played with them for hours and hours every day, and never seemed to tire of it. The more he got to know the girls, the prouder he became. He's a natural-born grandfather, but this of course doesn't surprise me in the least. It meant so much to me to have one of my parents meet my children for the very first time.

Through my dad's unbelievable joy, I could almost feel my mom's. It almost seemed like my mom was in the room, looking down on us, sporting one of her most fabulous scarves, surrounding us with her love and happiness. Finally, our brief few days were over and we said good-bye. I clung to my dad before he climbed into the taxi. For the first time, I felt really ready to go home.

❄⌇❄⌇❄

Today we are beginning the process of exiting India with our daughters. This is a bureaucratic nightmare that I have been dreading, particularly after the experience my German friends Arthur and Gilde had. What will happen if they won't grant us our visa for months? We both have businesses and lives to return to. I have had a passionate love affair with this place for the last few months, but now it's time to go home to real life, and to a certain extent, it's up to a bunch of nameless and faceless officials to decide if we get to return to our lives, or linger here in limbo, waiting for the red tape to resolve. I am praying, and chanting, and wishing that everything goes smoothly.

Fortunately, Alex is in a great mood this morning. He's dancing around the room. Alex always dances when he dresses in the morning, even at home. I love his lack of inhibition and sense of good fun. It's hilarious and charming and sexy all rolled up in one. I think he must have danced a lot as a little boy, and he doesn't get to do it nearly enough as a grown-up lawyer. But each morning, as he's pulling on his suit and tying his tie, he's all five-year-old. At least I know the girls will never want for entertainment or laughter. I'm glad they have a funny dad, just like I did.

I want the fun to last as long as possible because today is bound to be rough and exhausting. But I don't mention this to Alex. I don't want to dampen his spirits before the Indian red tape we are about to get tangled up in does it for me.

The challenge, Alyssa explained to me, is that in the smaller cities, such as Ahmedabad, they make up the laws as they go along. Mumbai is a bigger city with the U.S. Consulate near by. The officials in Mumbai process visas every day, so they are much less likely to get creative with the rules and regulations. In Ahmedabad, all bets are off.

We don't want to travel all the way to Mumbai with the girls in this heat, though, so we are taking our chances here. After a twenty-minute rickshaw ride, during which Alex thought he was going to die at least twice—amateur—we walk into a building that reeks of urine. We are told to go to the first floor. On the first floor, we are told to go to the ground floor. On the ground floor, we're told to go to the second floor. On the second floor, they don't have any idea what we're talking about. Okay, we're not off to a great start.

If I've learned anything in India, it's that one has to have patience. Become impatient and you destroy any possibility of making anything worthwhile happen. I take a deep breath. Thankfully, the girls are being good, even though the building is so hot and humid, the walls are practically sweating. I don't know how Arthur and Gilde have been able to do this for a full year. On the second floor, I walk into a room labeled "Pakistan." It looks like the room for presenting Pakistani visas, so we're getting warmer. Beyond this room is a room labeled "Foreigners." This is us.

A nice young Indian man smiles at me and asks what I want. I tell him that we need exit visas for our babies, who were born in India. He gives me a stack of papers to fill out and tells me to make various copies of our passports and our marriage license. Each form is three pages long. There are three sets for each of the two babies—in other words, this is too much to do here, holding babies who are becoming increasingly fussy. So we take the babies and the paperwork back to our hotel.

The next day, I tell Alex to stay home with the girls and I go back myself to the police commissioner's office with the eighteen forms, all filled out with care. The same nice guy reviews my paperwork and tells me that he's happy I took care in preparing the documents. I take this as a good sign. I notice that there isn't a paper clip or stapler in sight, at which point, the clerk punches a hole through my eighteen meticulous, handwritten pages with a screwdriver and then ties them together with thread. I think of the thread that Vaina gave me and smile.

Once our paperwork has been reviewed, I am interrogated by a police chief, who asks me why we didn't do this in America. Of course, it would have been impossible to get American passports for people who, as far as foreign diplomacy goes, did not yet exist, but I'm starting to wonder, why indeed! Then I'm told that we have to pay for the exist visas. The form says 1,650 rupees, but the police chief says that the fee is actually twice that amount. I don't argue.

I find the cashier, to whom I am supposed to pay the newly doubled fee. She tells me that I am too late for processing, even though I was told that the cashier's office closed at six, and it is now only three. The cashier sighs dramatically and shakes her head. Whether at the DMV in San Francisco or the cashier's station in India, why must all bureaucracy be uniformly frustrating? I continue to plead my case. She remains steadfast in her refusal to help me. I must return tomorrow at 10 a.m. to pay for processing. After this long day trapped in this dreary building, I am near my breaking point, so I play my last card: I need this processed today so that my newborn babies can get their exit visas.

At the mention of three-week-old twins, I can see her resolve instantly begin to soften. She tells me that I need to write down the serial number that appears on each bill so that she can confirm that I'm not using counterfeit bills. Because I look like such a criminal... unbelievable! I immediately lose my cool. I crack and start screaming at the top of my lungs, "Are you kidding me?! Seriously, you are going to make me do this? This is ridiculous! You and your system make no sense to me. Does this make you feel like you are doing your job well?" I stop myself as I realize I'm acting like a lunatic. I have been to a bank to withdraw funds, but even so, 3,300 rupees is a sizable stack of bills. Once I have finished, I hand her the bills and the piece of paper where I've recorded the bill numbers. Then I give her the babies' U.S. passports. She looks at the passports for a moment, and then suddenly slaps me across the face. Hard. My eyes fill with tears and my face flushes. I can feel the sting where her open hand struck me. I guess her insane slap was about her frustration in response to me. Not a love connection. But right now, I just want my exit visas. I will put up with anything, apparently, in order to get them. I touch my cheek, and the cashier silently begins to process the forms and tells me to go to the police commissioner's office in the morning with my husband and the girls. Apparently we all have to show our faces to finalize the visas. Ugh. I had the feeling she slapped me because I kept giving her rude looks, the result of me having been exhausted, sweating like a pig, and basically at my wits' end. I believe this was her way of saying "I have the power here." I also think that she might have had a bit of an anti-surrogacy bias, based on her response to me. But who knows for sure?

Alex recalled Abhi's recommendation of getting the exit

visas in Mumbai because there could be "problems" in the more provincial Ahmedabad. At this point filing a complaint or con^ fronting a bureaucrat would do nothing more than add further delay, and might even cause more serious complications. More^ over, the Ahmedabad police station felt more like a military base, especially after the terrorist bombings just ten months be^ fore; there were guard towers, armored cars, security gates, and men with machine guns. This was not a place that had a "com^ plaints" box.

Alex asked me if, for the time being, I would be willing to swallow my pride and let the incident go. I could always write a complaint letter on the plane. After everything we had been through, letting it go was actually the smallest of sacrifices to make. And in the end, I never wrote any letter because by the time we were over the Atlantic all of these little bumps in the road had faded from memory.

The next day, Alex and I show up to prove that we are who we say we are, and end up waiting all day long, again, in a dank cement building with little ventilation and little to keep the girls, or us, occupied, nourished, or hydrated. The girls are get^ ting increasingly fussy. We couldn't bring bottles with us, and we forgot pacifiers at the hotel. We bounce the babies like they have never been bounced before, cooing, singing, showering them with attention, all the time waiting to be called. The wait is interminable.

Finally, an officer brings us into a small room. He asks us a few basic questions and tells us to come back tomorrow. I feel like I may begin to start sobbing right here in this damp inter^ rogation room. How many days is this going to go on? Are we going to wind up like Arthur and Gilde? I have done everything that they asked of me, and right now, I just want to be able to take my daughters home. Really, truly, *home*, not to another hotel room. I want to be near my father, my sister, my friends, and I want to get out of this room so badly, I could scream. I take a deep breath, which at least is a real option.

The next morning, with the girls and their pacifiers, we go back to the police commissioner's office. Thankfully, a good night's sleep, away from the creaking bureaucracy of Ahmedabad, has lifted my spirits. Today I greet the old man behind the counter with a smile. He glares at me, but then, a small miracle happens. He pulls out an ancient stamp and starts stamping enthusiastically—eight stamps on each piece of paper for each baby. He writes the date next to each stamp and explains that we must leave the country within ten days of the date on the stamp. I can't believe that we have finally done the impossible—we can leave!—and that our exit from this country is finally legitimate. We are going to go home.

The next day, after Alex and I have secured flights out of India and back to San Francisco, we have one more good-bye to say.

"Hello, Atreff," says Hitesh, who is going to take me to his home for the last time. Dr. Patel is throwing a party for us and for Caroline and Cyril tonight. Their twins were released from the NICU soon after my girls were, and they are returning home to London tomorrow morning.

"Hello, Hitesh," I say, "It's so nice to see you again. Thank you for driving all this way to get me."

"No problem! It's a special day. Your last visit to our bar, heh, Hadreen?"

"Yes," I say wistfully, and Alex shakes his head and smiles. He has gotten used to Hitesh's sense of humor. "I don't know how we will ever say good-bye to you two, or to Anand."

"Not good bye," says Hitesh meaningfully. "Only until the next time we meet." He puts the pedal to the metal, propelling us into the familiar crush of traffic.

When we arrive, we walk once again up the lovely stone walkway into the Patels' beautiful home. We pass the prayer room where Dr. Patel prays for her patients every day, and out onto the vast lawn where Caroline and Cyril are sitting with Dr. Patel in the friendly old Gujarati swing, the same one I used to take in a little fresh air during those tedious editing sessions. The book is now available, and used as a promotional tool for patients to learn about surrogacy when talking to Dr. Patel and considering the services of the Akanksha Clinic.

"Congratulations, Adrienne and Alex," says Dr. Patel, hugging us.

"Thank you," I say, welling up. "I don't know what we would have ever done without you." Dr. Patel smiles and staves off the burgeoning tide of my tears with a warm laugh and a kiss on the cheek. Then we all sit around and have cocktails, and eat Dr. Patel's spicy peanuts, and talk about babies, just as brandnew parents do all over the world.

At the end of the night, when it's finally time to say good night, there are no tears. There is instead an outpouring of warmth, and gratitude and promises to see each other again one day soon.

※ ❧※❧ ※

In the morning, we fly to a place called Elsewhere, in Goa, which is heavenly. After spending the first ten weeks of the babies' lives in humid heat, it is nearly indescribable what it feels like when the breeze dances across my skin and blows back my hair. But I'll try: it's glorious.

In Anand, we had been careful to keep the girls inside, closest to whichever air-conditioner happened to be working at the moment, and away from the dirt and the noise of the crowded streets. Here in Goa, by the sea, they are safe from the heat and the mosquitoes. The sun and salty fresh air really do wonders for the soul, as well as everything else. The babies finally reach six pounds, which is the goal weight that both Dr. Patel and our American pediatrician recommend before traveling. They are thriving and adorable. India continues to be feisty, while Emma is more subdued. Aside from having a bottle of formula handy when they're hungry, Alex and I don't have a care in the world. Our days are filled with surf and sand, babies, and bottle. Kristi joined us, and she tells me that she has never been to the sea before. Here in the silence of Goa, she can hear herself pray. She says she feels like a changed person.

I could have stayed forever.

But, after seven heavenly days in Goa, we return to Ahmedabad. We are just one step away from San Francisco. I pack all of the babies' things last. Traveling with small children, as any parent knows, is stressful and anxiety-inducing, and with the babies being so small, I am simply concerned that Alex and I have enough diapers, clean bottles, formula, blankets, baby wipes, cloths, pacifiers, etc., etc., for the impending flights. There are so many germs in airports and circulated through a plane's cabin; I pack baby Tylenol and a thermometer in case they catch something while traveling.

The car picks us up right on time, which is encouraging and unusual. We are flying first to Mumbai, then after a layover we'll go directly to San Francisco. I hope the girls can make it; I hope my nerves will make it. Kristi holds the girls while Alex and I help the driver with our luggage. She hands Emma and India to us, and I feel incredibly sad to leave yet another friend here. After a tearful good-bye, my family and I settle into the back of our taxi and head to the airport.

At immigration we proudly deposit our three copies and three-inch stack of visas and notarized documents. The officer gamely thumbs through them for less than a minute, stamps everything loudly, and ushers us along.

The girls are, thankfully, asleep through the short flight to Mumbai and are most active while we are still in the airport. A constant business traveler myself, I know how hated parents of crying children are on long flights! I know that they will calm down for a nice long sleep on the plane home. Once we finally board, the anxiety and stress I've been feeling for the past few days finally evaporates. I sink into my seat. I will carry India home, and Alex will carry Emma.

What an unbelievable journey this has been. Three years ago, I was mourning the loss of yet another pregnancy, and today I am the mother of beautiful twin girls. This path to parenthood has been fraught and is not for the faint of heart, but I found so many wonderful friends and supportive physicians along the way. It has been a truly miraculous journey.

India murmurs and curls her warm body into my chest. Alex grabs my hand, and I am filled with emotion. In my other hand, as I feel us lift off and head westward into our future, I grip the strings that Vaina has given me. I am sad to leave this place and those people whom I have grown to love, but I do not mourn. I know that one day we will be back, and that no matter how far apart we are geographically, Vaina, my daughters, and I will always be connected by this sacred thread.

EPILOGUE

one year later

Abhi and I bounce along the dirt road toward a small Muslim village in a corner of Gujarat that I have never been before. I wonder if *any* Westerners have been here before. It is so secluded, only those who know it is there could ever find it. Abhi, with his usual automotive magic, parts a sea of shepherds and sheep that briefly overwhelm the road, which looks more like a winding dirt path to nowhere. *Oh my God, I'm back in India.*

"I hope we don't run out of gas," I say to Abhi, looking at the vast expanse of endless fields all around me. There are definitely no gas stations. No Triple A. No convenience stores to get a soda and wait for help. Nothing but sheep and cows and the men who tend them.

"No worries, Atreen. You know Abhi always gets you where you are going safe and sound," he says reassuringly. "We will be there very soon." I feel those familiar butterflies in my stomach, the same ones I felt right before I first met Vaina.

Ever since leaving India, I've thought constantly of coming back. There is something about this place that grounds me, that reminds me of what is essential, and separates the substance from the noise. My life has been a symphony of bottles and bassinets, and juggling two careers while learning how to be the parents of adorable twins. My life is everything that I had ever hoped it would be. But something is missing. Some*one* is missing. And that someone is Vaina.

I'm envious of people I know who did surrogacy closer to home. They can have lunch with their surrogates, show them pictures of the babies, and regularly refresh and nurture the special ties that bind them. I've written to Vaina many times over the last year and sent pictures of the twins as they leap over each new developmental hurdle. I send the letters through Dr. Patel as I've been instructed, but I never hear back. I have no idea if she's received them. Honestly, I don't know how she would, deep in the Gujarati outback, where mail trucks fear to tread. I've rung the cell phone I gave her several times, but I've never gotten an answer. I wonder if they sold the phone. Or maybe it's just never turned on.

When I first began my surrogacy journey, the idea that I would never see my surrogate again comforted me. I liked the idea that the whole adventure could be worlds away, if I chose. But I forgot there was a flip side to that coin. Vaina would be worlds away, even if I chose to reach out to her.

So, here I am, in India. The twins are still too young for this adventure, so I left them home alone with their father for the very first time. He seemed elated at the prospect. And of course, our nanny has strict instructions to keep all three of them in line until I get home. That is, if I get home. If there is such a place as a point of no return, I think I must be very close to it. The Indian music blasting from Abhi's car radio suddenly goes silent. It's so remote here, there isn't even a radio signal. No wonder Vaina hasn't answered my calls; there can't possibly be cell service out here.

I set up the appointment through Dr. Patel, although whether or not Vaina even knows I'm coming is questionable. I don't doubt Dr. Patel, but the concept of schedules and appointments doesn't hold a lot of weight in India. It's another one of the lessons I've come to relearn. You can't plan for life, you just have to live it.

Finally I see a cluster of ramshackle houses grouped together at the base of a small hill, masked by lush trees. I can almost see people moving about inside the tiny enclave. This must be Vaina's village. I had imagined what her world looked like, but now that I'm seeing it, it's alarming. It's not that I expected something different, not entirely, but seeing her actual home rather than the one I imagined gives me an entirely new perspective on just how different our worlds truly are.

We park the car outside the entrance to the village and walk in on foot.

"Why are we leaving the car here?" I ask Abhi, putting both feet down somewhat tentatively in this completely unfamiliar territory.

"No parking in there," says Abhi, who I suspect is worried about his car. We haven't passed another one in at least one hundred miles. A car driving on the road here is as much a spectacle to these people as the first elephant I saw walking through the streets of Anand had been to me. I don't have any idea how Vaina was even able to get to the clinic.

Once we walk into the village, I understand the wisdom of Abhi's plan. Even on foot, I feel like the president. People are taking snapshots of me—there may not be cars, but there are enough cameras for me to feel like a victim of paparazzi—or videotaping me as I walk by. Everyone comes out onto their porches, or stops dead in their tracks to stare at the crazy white lady, in the ridiculous hat, who has suddenly strolled into their village. The car would have been total overkill.

We reach a small, well-kept home at the end of the lane, and walk up the few steps to the entrance. Vaina comes out of her door and rushes toward me. Her three children tag along behind her, and we embrace. It feels so good to put my arms around her.

"Hello, Hadrin, I missed you," she says and holds my hand the way she used to when we passed those quiet hours together in the surrogate house.

"Hello, Vaina. I missed you too," I say, and I let her lead me into her home.

It feels like no time has passed. Vaina is wearing a beautiful white sari, and her head is covered, in traditional Muslim fashion. She looks so happy, in her element, with her children laughing and playing all around her. The anxiety of pressing poverty has been lifted from her shoulders, I can tell. She looks completely at ease, and so does her whole family. The relief even extends beyond her front doors, because in Muslim cultures, the wealth is often shared. I saw a school being built as I walked into town; I wonder if Vaina's surrogacy fee is helping to make this school possible.

Vaina leads me into the main room, which is a large, tiled gathering place with virtually no furniture. I greet her husband as well as her brother-in-law, and his family. We all sit down on the floor. We make for quite an eclectic circle. If you were looking from afar, you would say that I was the one person who doesn't belong in this picture. Yet somehow, I know that I very much do.

Vaina and I belong together, although just quite how or why continues to elude me. Those months together taught me how peaceful it is to sit still, to be quiet, and to watch things grow. She is the one who gave me a new reason to be amazed and grateful at the gifts I have been given with the dawn of every new day. We are forever connected, she and I. When I'm with her, I feel like I'm at home. And I think she feels the same way about me.

They serve me Coke, which is a delicacy in these parts, with fried potatoes, which is also a rare treat, reserved for Western visitors. This is not the first Indian home I've been in where they offered me this interesting cultural homage. What do you serve an American? Coke and french fries, of course.

"How have you been doing?" I ask her, as Abhi translates. "How is nursing school?"

"No nursing school," Vaina says. "My husband bought a taxi, and my brother-in-law has a good business now that he started with some of the money."

"That's great," I say. I had hoped that just as I had absorbed the wisdom of sitting still and dwelling in the moment, perhaps Vaina might have absorbed some of the wisdom of being an independent woman.

"I will do surrogacy again," she says to me, and I realize that, in fact, Vaina has found a marketable skill that allows her to be an independent woman. Before she found Dr. Patel, she had sewn beads on saris or, for a brief stint, was a housecleaner. Both jobs are tedious, exhausting, and pay very poorly. Being a surrogate pays better and fits more realistically into her lifestyle. After all those nights working with the Anand writers' circle, I now understand Dr. Patel's passion about removing the stigma from surrogacy. It allows women like Vaina to do the good work that they do, with respect and honor, as they deserve.

"Why don't you have more babies?" she says to me and smiles and winks a little, being playful with me. But I can see she's quite serious. "I could be surrogate again. We are friends, Hadrin. I don't want you to leave. I love you."

"You did the best job ever and I will forever be grateful for what you have done for us," I say and squeeze her hand, welcoming her affection, but letting her know, two babies and one adventure in surrogacy is quite enough for me. Her husband says something suddenly that I don't understand, and Vaina says something back to him somewhat sternly, which I suspect is something along the lines of "Be quiet, you idiot."

I look at her husband, and realize that he is wearing a cast.

"What happened to your arm?" I ask him, and Vaina explains that her husband has wrecked his cab and broken his arm. I realize now what the husband must have been saying, and why Vaina is so anxious for our family to grow again. Her husband needs a new cab.

I have been planning on giving Vaina a gift, but I hadn't expected to give it to her in front of her entire family. I want her to know that we still think and care about her from afar. I hand a small bag of gifts for her and her family of clothing, chocolate, photos of the girls, Alex, and me, and an envelope of money.

"For your kids' education," I say. Vaina and her husband both erupt into bright smiles, and Vaina squeezes my hand and calls her children over.

"Tell Hadrin what you learned," she says in English and her children giggle shyly and hide behind their mother.

"I like San Francisco," says one of her sons.

"I like New York and America and Angelina Jolie," says her daughter.

"That's great!" I say. Vaina beams at me, proud that she has taught her children about a little piece of my world.

We spend the rest of the day holding hands and watching the children play, and choking down fried potatoes. Before I know it, it's time to leave, and once again I don't know how to say good-bye. We are forever connected by the sacred thread of our respect for each other, and our love for these children. It will never be good-bye, but rather, a temporary parting until we meet again.

ACKNOWLEDGMENTS

I am grateful for all the help I had in writing this book—the brains, emotions, creativity, and energy it took was enormous.

I would like to thank Beverly West, fearless writing partner extraordinaire, Jason Allen Ashlock, literary agent of the digital age, and my editors, Kate Kennedy and Jenna Ciongoli, who believed in my story and willed it into being an actual book about the difficult journey I went through to become a mother. Their care on this very personal journey was critical in my finishing the book. I am grateful to be able to share my story with other couples that struggle with infertility.

Along the way the following people helped me tremendously and I am proud to call them my friends: Sasha Lazard and Regina George, for the constant text messages, inspiration to continue writing, and belief in this book. Maja Smith for always being my spiritual light. Sora Lee for discovering India with me on my first trip and for being just you. Michelle Clark for bossing me around to get this done. Andrew Miller for your first words on the book (and teardrop) about chapter 1. Alexandra Palmer for always making me feel like I could do anything. Dorka Keehn for forcing me to use my brain. Matthew Haimes for always raising the bar on what friendship means. Nicole Needham, Erica Gragg, Lydia Wendt, Elizabeth Roberts, Catherine Chow, Natalia Seidel, Chelsea Ialeggio, Jason Mitchell, Sarah Takesh, Aimee Logan, Kristin Fiore, Kelly Fair, Irene Edwards, Caroline Cameron, and Emma

Acknowledgments

Pilkington for the beautiful cards, emails, and constant words of encouragement.

My family—my father, Allen (you really are the best father in the world), my sister, Allison (my sibling soul mate), my late mother, Carol, for teaching me how to really care about what is important, my stepmother, Patricia (you are a treasure in my world), and my in-laws, Michael and Jenny. And, of course, my love, Alex, who pushed, encouraged, grammatically corrected, and cheered me to the finish. I love you.

And finally, a thank-you to Pete's Coffee for helping me wake up a bit earlier to write each morning.

RESOURCES

Two and a half years have passed since the birth of my twin girls, and I continue to learn more about foreign surrogacy. My humble advice is that anyone entering into a relationship with a surrogate, whether domestically or abroad, should strive to be as passionate an advocate for the health and well-being of the surrogate as you are for yourself and your children. Legal and medical regulations regarding egg donation, IVF, and surrogacy vary from state to state and country to country and are constantly in flux and evolving. While consulting with legal and medical professionals is in one's best interest, it is imperative to be an educated client. Do your homework researching the clinic, the doctors, the program, and, most important, your surrogate.

These are resources that I found particularly helpful as I researched foreign gestational surrogacy, but it is certainly not an exhaustive list.

AllAboutSurrogacy.com
Open forum to discuss surrogacy

CircleSurrogacy.com
Information for surrogacy in the United States

www.IVFcharotar.com
This is the clinic I went to.

http://web.creaworld.org/
CREA empowers women and girls to articulate and access their human rights by enhancing women's leadership in India.

PlanetHospital.net
Resource for finding clinics abroad

IndiaAdoption.com
A useful guide on the process